Mac OS X
KillerTips

Scott Kelby

MAC OS X V. 10.2 JAGUAR KILLER TIPS

The Mac OS X v. 10.2 Jaguar
Killer Tips Team

EDITOR
Richard Theriault

TECHNICAL EDITOR
Chris Main

PRODUCTION EDITOR
Kim Gabriel

PRODUCTION
Dave Damstra

CAPTURES
Tommy Maloney

COVER DESIGN AND
CREATIVE CONCEPTS
Felix Nelson

SITE DESIGN
Stacy Behan

The New Riders Team

PUBLISHER
David Dwyer

ASSOCIATE PUBLISHER
Stephanie Wall

EXECUTIVE EDITOR
Steve Weiss

MANAGING EDITOR
Sarah Kearns

PRODUCTION
Wil Cruz

PROOFREADER
Linda Seifert

PUBLISHED BY
New Riders Publishing

Copyright © 2003 by Scott Kelby

FIRST EDITION: September 2002

International Standard Book Number: 0-7357-1317-0

Library of Congress Catalog Card Number: 2002106395

06 05 04 03 02 7 6 5 4 3 2 1

Interpretation of the printing code: The rightmost double-digit number is the year of the book's printing; the rightmost single-digit number is the number of the book's printing. For example, the printing code 02-1 shows that the first printing of the book occurred in 2002.

Composed in Myriad, Trebuchet, and Minion by NAPP Publishing

Printed in the United States of America

Trademarks

Warning and Disclaimer

www.newriders.com
www.scottkelbybooks.com

For my amazing wife, Kalebra

"You don't marry someone you can live with.

You marry the person you cannot live without."

—UNKNOWN

ACKNOWLEDGMENTS

Although only one person's name winds up on the spine of this book, it takes a large army of people to put out a book, and without their help, dedication, and tireless efforts, there wouldn't even have been a spine; and to them I'm greatly indebted.

First, I want to thank absolutely just the coolest person I've ever met—my wife, Kalebra. I don't know how I ever got lucky enough to marry her nearly 14 years ago, but it was without a doubt the smartest thing I've ever done, and the greatest blessing God's ever given me. She just flat-out rocks, and at this point, I can't imagine that the crush I've had on her since the first time I met her will ever go away. I love you, Sweetie!

Secondly, I want to thank my son Jordan. Little Buddy—there's so much of your mom in you, in particular her kind, loving heart, and that's about the best head start anyone could ask for in life. You're the greatest little guy in the world, and thanks so much for making me smile every single day while I was writing this book, and for letting me play Rescue Heroes with you on your iMac.

I want to thank my team at KW Media Group—they're a unique group of people, with limitless energy and amazing talent, and I'd put them up against anybody in the business. In particular, I want to thank my Creative Director Felix Nelson for his great ideas, cool cover designs, and intro artwork, and for his ongoing dedication to creating a quality product. I want to thank my Tech Editor Chris Main for making sure everything works the way it should, and for never letting me slide anything by him. I want to thank the amazing layout master Dave Damstra for making the book look so squeaky clean, my Production Editor Kim Gabriel for making sure everything came together on time, my editing and design crew Barbara Thompson, Margie Rosenstein, and Ted LoCascio, and my friend Dave Moser for his unwavering commitment to making sure that everything we do is better than what we've done before. Carry on, soldier. Thanks to Tommy Maloney for his dedication and all his great help with the book's graphics, and to Stacy Behan for coolly handling the Web side of things.

I'm really delighted to be working once again with my original editor at *Mac Today* magazine, Richard "Dicky" Theriault. He's an absolute joy to work with, and he knows the Mac market, and the people in it, inside and out. His help, input, guidance, and friendship are very important, and warmly appreciated.

I want to thank my friends and business partners Jim Workman and Jean Kendra for their support and enthusiasm for all my writing projects, and Pete Kratzenberg for making it all add up. I also want to thank my brother Jeff for his letting me constantly "pick his brain," and for his many ideas, input, support, hard work, and most of all for just being such a great brother to me always.

Of course, I couldn't do any of it without the help of my wonderful assistant Kathy Siler, and all the "behind-the-scenes" team at KW, including Lawrence Atkinson, John Podelski, and Cathy Oliver in shipping; Rosemarie Alleva and her crew: Maureen Arms, Amanda McCormack, Chris Thomas, Rita Hargrove, and Diane Brisson; and thanks and much love go to Julie Stephenson and Ronni "Miss Ronni" O'Neil. My thanks go to Sarah Hughes, Scott Stahley, Mike Donadio, Kristin Kirby, Melinda Gotelli, Rick Tracewell, and Sandureen Stoker. Also thanks to Barbie Taylor for joining our team (and for helping me find Kathy Siler). I also want to give my personal thanks to Gina Profitt and Tameka Thomas. They may be gone, but they're not forgotten.

I want to thank all my "Mac Buddies" who've taught me so much over the years, including Bill Carroll, Jim Goodman, Dick Theriault, Don Wiggins, Dave Gales, Jim Patterson, Larry Becker, Jim Workman, Jon Gales, Jim Nordquist, and a big thanks to my buddy Rod "Mac Daddy" Harlan (President of the DVPA) for his contribution of some very cool iDVD tips.

I want to include a special thank you to renowned Macintosh author David Pogue. It was his book *Mac OS X: The Missing Manual* that really got me excited about Mac OS X, and I think it's absolutely the best book written on the subject—period (and believe me, I've read them all)!

Thanks to Steve Weiss and everyone at New Riders, for letting me "drop this book in," for their ongoing commitment to excellence, and for the honor of letting me be one of their "Voices that Matter."

And most importantly, an extra special thanks to God and Jesus Christ for always hearing my prayers, for always being there when I need Him, and for blessing me with a wonderful life I truly love, and such a warm loving family to share it with.

Scott Kelby

Scott is Editor-in-Chief and co-founder of *Mac Design Magazine,* Editor-in-Chief of *Photoshop User* magazine, and president of the National Association of Photoshop Professionals, the trade association for Adobe® Photoshop® users. Scott is also president of KW Media Group, Inc., a Florida-based software training and publishing firm.

Scott is author of the books *Macintosh: The Naked Truth, Photoshop 7 Down & Dirty Tricks, Photoshop Photo-Retouching Secrets,* and *Photoshop 7 Killer Tips*, all from New Riders Publishing. He's a contributing author to the books *Photoshop 6 Effects Magic,* also from New Riders; *Maclopedia, the Ultimate Reference on Everything Macintosh* from Hayden Books; and *Adobe Web Design and Publishing Unleashed* from Sams.net Publishing.

Scott is training director for the Adobe Photoshop Seminar Tour, technical chair for PhotoshopWorld (the annual convention for Adobe Photoshop users), and a speaker at graphics trade shows and events around the world. Scott is also featured in a series of Adobe Photoshop video training tapes and CD-ROMs and has been training graphics professionals since 1993.

Scott lives in the Tampa Bay area of Florida with his wife, Kalebra, and his son, Jordan. For more background info, visit www.scottkelby.com.

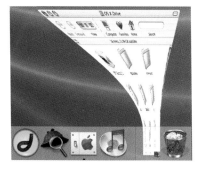

TABLE OF CONTENTS

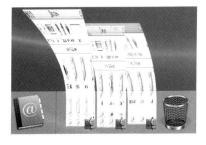

TABLE OF CONTENTS

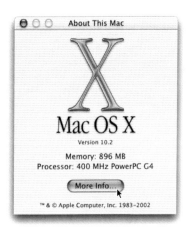

TABLE OF CONTENTS

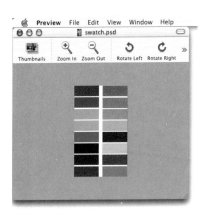

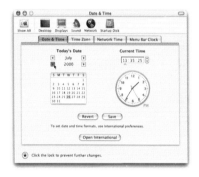

TABLE OF CONTENTS

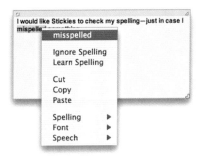

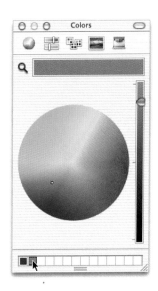

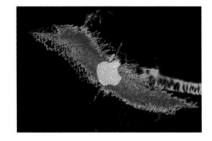

TABLE OF CONTENTS

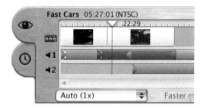

WARNING:
AS MANY AS 7% OF THE PEOPLE
WHO START HERE WILL SUFFER
SPONTANEOUS BLINDNESS

Wait a minute. Is this just a scam to get me to read the book's introduction?

Honestly? Yes. That's exactly what it is, so don't worry; 7% of you aren't going to experience spontaneous blindness. It's really more like 4%. I hate to resort to this kind of hyperbole just to get you to read the introduction but because this is a totally different kind of Mac book, it's really important that you fully read the introduction (and it wouldn't hurt if you memorized each paragraph, including punctuation, just in case). Look, it's only like three pages long, and quickly reading it will answer a lot of your questions, help you to get the most out of the book, and lead you to a true and lasting inner peace that only comes from becoming "one" with the introduction. Let us begin.

What exactly is a Killer Tip book?

There are two types of people in this world: (1) the type of people who want to understand everything before they do anything. These are the people who buy a new computer, read the entire instruction manual, inventory all the packing items, and only when they feel certain that they have a full and complete understanding of the entire project before them, do they actually remove the styrofoam cover and pull their new Mac out of the shipping carton. There are no more than 17 of these people using Macs in the world today. This book is not for them.

This book is for (2) the rest of us. People who buy a Mac, tear open the box, set it all up, turn it on, and start messin' around with it. These same people eventually buy computer books, and while casually flipping through them, they stop to read all the sidebar tips first. These are people like you and me. (Well, at least like me, anyway.) I'm an absolute sucker for sidebar tips. I'm hooked on 'em, and whenever I buy a new computer book, the first thing I do is read all those cool little tips littered throughout the sidebars. Sometimes they're in boxes with a tinted background (like the one shown on the left), sometimes they're on the side of the page, sometimes at the bottom—it doesn't matter—if it says the word tip—I'm drawn to it like an attorney to a slip-and-fall injury in a Vegas casino.

I finally figured out why I like sidebar tips so much—it's where the "really cool stuff" is. Think about it, if you were writing a computer book and you've got some really ingenious technique, some really great undocumented keyboard shortcut, or a closely guarded inside secret you to want to share with your readers—you want it to stand out and yell, "Hey, there's a very cool thing right over here!" You're not going to bury it inside paragraphs of techno-text. This is exciting stuff. It's intriguing. It's fun. So, you pull it out

TIP

This is a sidebar tip. Every great Mac book has a few of them. But this book is nothing but them. A whole book of cool sidebar tips. Without the sidebars.

from the regular text, slap a border around it, add a tint behind it, and maybe even add a special graphic to get the reader's attention. It works. The only problem with sidebar tips is—there's just not enough of 'em.

So I got to thinkin', "Wouldn't it be cool if there was a book where the whole book, cover-to-cover, was nothing but those little sidebar tips? No long paragraphs explaining the Hierarchical File System. No detailed descriptions of how to configure a LAN, or sixteen ways to partition your hard drive—just the fun stuff—just the tips. Well, that's exactly what this is—a book of nothing but Mac OS X sidebar tips. Without the sidebars.

So what exactly is a "Killer Tip?"

"Double-click on a folder to open it." Technically, that is a tip. It's a very lame tip. It's a boringly obvious tip, and it's definitely not a Killer Tip. If it's a "Killer Tip" it makes you "nod and smile" when you read it, and you'll be nodding and smiling so much in this book, you're going to look like "a bobbing dog" in the rear window of a Buick Park Avenue. (I used a Buick Park Avenue as an example because it has a big enough rear window that you can climb up there yourself to test out my prediction. See, I care.) The goal here is to give you tips that are so cool, that after reading just a few you have to pick up the phone, call your Mac buddies, and totally tune them up with your newfound Mac OS X power.

Is this book for you?

Is this book for you? Are you kidding? This book is *so* for you that if you're reading this in a bookstore, and you don't have the money to buy it, you'll shoplift it—risking possible incarceration—just to unlock the secrets its coated pages hold. But you won't have to shoplift it, because if you're reading a Macintosh book, you bought a Macintosh computer, and that probably means you have lots of money. So buy at least two copies.

Look, although I don't know you personally, I'm willing to bet you love those little sidebar tips just as much as I do. If you didn't, authors would've stopped adding them to their books years ago. But as much as you love those sidebar tips, you still want something more. That's right—you want visuals. As cool as those sidebar tips are, they're usually just a tiny little box with a couple of lines of text (like the sidebar shown at left). So in this book, I thought I'd expand the explanations just enough to make them more accessible, and then add an accompanying screen capture if (a) it helps make the tip easier to understand, or (b) if the page just looks really boring without them.

Is there any UNIX? It scares me.

Mac OS X is built on UNIX, but don't worry—it pretty much stays out of your way. Here's a way to think of it: The pilots of commercial airliners use engines to fly the plane, right? But if they want to start the engines, they don't climb out on each wing and manually crank them up—they do it from up in the cockpit with a flick of a switch. That's kind of like Mac OS X's relationship with UNIX. You're up front in the cockpit running things, you push Macintosh buttons, and UNIX responds (quite brilliantly, I might add), without you having to get your hands dirty.

The vast majority of people who use Mac OS X will never mess with its UNIX "soul" directly (by "mess with," I mean altering their system by writing UNIX command lines. It's not for the faint of heart, because in some cases if you make a mistake while coding, you can seriously mess up your Mac). That's why I decided not to include UNIX tips in the book—I didn't want to have a situation where the vast majority of the book's readers would see a UNIX chapter and go, "Oh, that's not for me." I wanted everybody to have the chance to use every single tip, in every single chapter. However, if you're really into the UNIX side of Mac OS X, I didn't want to leave you out altogether, so I put some of my favorite UNIX tips on the book's companion Web site just for you, at www.scottkelbybooks.com/macosxkillertips/scaryunixstuff.html.

What about that whole .Mac thing?

In an incredibly popular move, Apple did away with their free iTools service and replaced it with an expensive pay service called .Mac. (Note: It was only incredibly popular with Apple executives, who immediately had to raise the drawbridge to keep the angry villagers from torching their castle.) I have to say this (1) the .Mac thing is pretty cool, but (2) I've yet to meet a single iTools user who says they're going to pay for the .Mac service (although I'm sure some people will. Primarily rich slumlords). The .Mac online service is designed to integrate with Mac OS X, but since it's not part of Mac OS X itself, I didn't include any .Mac stuff in the book. Again, it would have created a chapter that most of you would've skipped (except for millionaire CEO types, professional ball players, Hollywood producers, real estate moguls, etc.).

Okay, how do I get started?

My books aren't set up like a novel—you can jump in anywhere and start on any page. That's true for all of my books, with the notable exception of *Macintosh: The Naked Truth*, which is about what life is really like being a Mac user in a PC-dominated world. I'm not going to try to plug that book here (ISBN 0-7357-1284-0 from New Riders Publishing. $19.99. Found anywhere cool Mac books are sold) because that's just tacky (Amazon.com offers discounts on the book—order yours today). Well, with this book you don't have to start at Chapter 1 and read your way through to the back (although there's nothing wrong with that). Actually, you can start in any chapter and immediately try the tips that interest you the most. Also, don't forget to read each chapter's intro page—it's critical to your understanding of what's in that particular chapter (that's totally not true, but it took me a long time to write those intros, so I use little lies like that to get you to read them. Sad, isn't it?).

Wait! One last thing!

I want to let you know, before you go any further, that the only three sidebar tip "boxes" in the entire book appear in the sidebars of this introduction. So, don't go looking for them because (as I said) the book is made up of sidebar tips *without* the sidebars. Okay tiger— I'm cuttin' you loose. It's time to go get "tipsy."

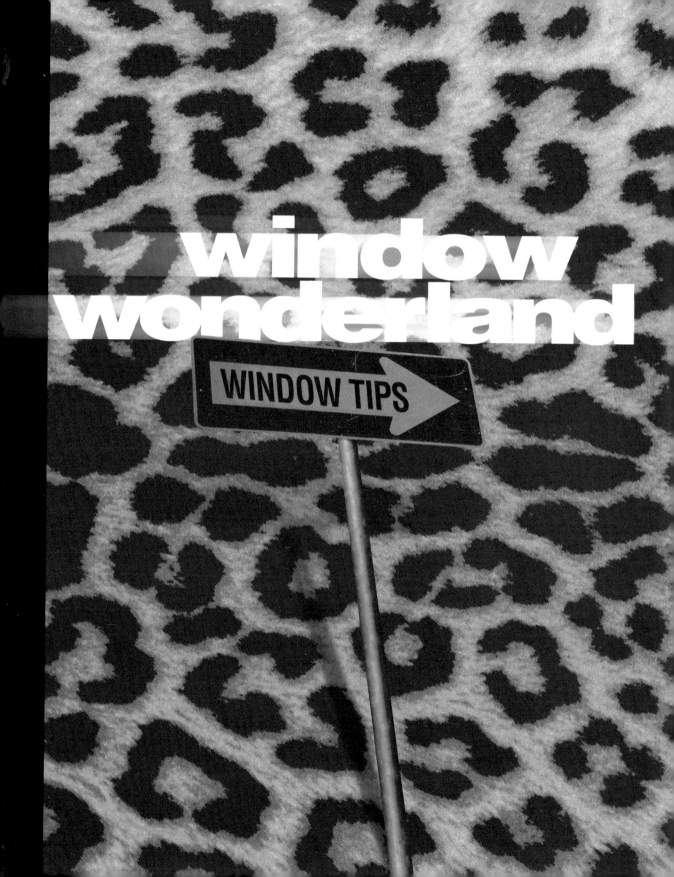

window wonderland

WINDOW TIPS

I have to be honest with you. I have some major concerns about the subhead for this chapter "Cool Window Tips." My fear is that you might

Window Wonderland
cool window tips

give it a quick glance and accidentally read it as "Cool Windows Tips" which this chapter, in a Mac OS X book, clearly is not. It fact, this couldn't be a chapter on Microsoft Windows, primarily because I don't know Windows. Well, I know where the Start menu is, and I can launch an application (if it's fairly easy to find) but that's as much as I'm willing to admit (at least without a Congressional subpoena). Besides, how could there be anything cool about Windows? So what is this chapter really about? I was hoping you would know. Hmmmm. This is kind of embarrassing. Okay, I'll take a stab at it—it sounds like it's probably filled with tips on using Finder windows, managing your files within them, and other cool window tips that will amuse your friends and absolutely captivate small children and family pets (except, of course, for fish, which are waiting patiently for you to overfeed them).

   SPEED TIP: FASTER FULL-NAME VIEWING IN LIST VIEW

When you're looking for files in either List
View or Column View, it's almost certain that
some of your files with long names will have
some of their letters (or even full words) cut
off from view. There is a tip that will save you
from having to resize your List or Column View
columns—just hold your cursor over the file's
truncated name for a few seconds and eventually its full name will pop up. So what's the
problem? The "few seconds" part. Instead,
hold the Option key, *then* put your cursor
over the file's name, and its full name will
appear instantly.

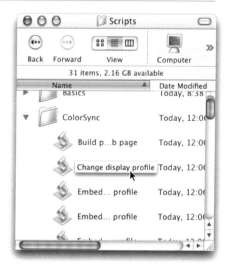

   SPEED TIP: DELETING FILES VIA THE TOOLBAR

Want to delete (trash) a file with extreme prejudice? You can use the old Mac OS 9
shortcut of clicking on the file and pressing Command-Delete, which puts it on the
express lane to the Trash, but another thing you can do is to add the "Delete" icon right
to your Toolbar. Then you can click on a file, and click the Delete icon for a one-way
ticket to the Trash. You do that by going under the View menu and choosing Customize
Toolbar. When the dialog appears, you'll see the Delete icon (the red circle with a
diagonal line through it). Drag that up to the Toolbar, and now it's right there, ready for
the clicking (just remember to click on the file you want to delete first before you click
the Delete icon).

MOVING WINDOWS BEHIND YOUR CURRENT WINDOW

This is a really handy tip for
"window overload" while you're
working in the Finder. If you're
working within a window, you can
actually move non-active windows
that appear behind it. Just hold
the Command key and click and
drag their titlebar to move them
(even though you're moving them,
it doesn't bring them to front or
make them active). Better yet, if
you want to minimize or close any
of these "windows in the back,"
you don't even have to hold the

Command key: just move your cursor over their inactive Close, Minimize, or Zoom
buttons on the left-hand side of the titlebar, and they become active (they will appear
in their usual red, yellow, and green).

   COLUMN VIEW'S HIDDEN POWER

One of the coolest benefits of Column
View (the third choice from the left in the
Toolbar's View icon) is that, depending on
the file, you can see a preview of its
contents (at least if it's a photo, MP3
audio file, or a QuickTime movie). This is
especially helpful if you're searching for a
QuickTime movie, because if you click on
a movie while in Column View, a large
thumbnail showing the first frame of the
movie appears in the far right column.
But more importantly, the QuickTime
Player controls appear just below the
thumbnail. To see the movie, right there
in the Column View (without having to
launch the full QuickTime Player), just
click on the Play button.

CAN'T SEE ENOUGH IN COLUMN VIEW? STRETCH IT

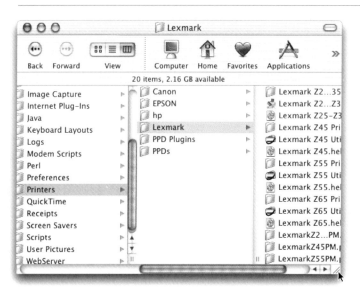

If you're working in a Finder window and you find yourself scrolling and scrolling with the bottom scrollbar to get to the files you need, stop the madness. Instead, just grab the bottom-right corner of the window and stretch it out to the right to make the rest of the columns visible.

ADJUSTING JUST ONE COLUMN IN COLUMN VIEW

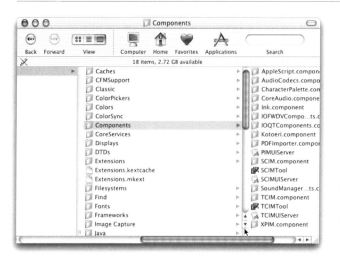

As we showed in the previous tip, when you're in Column View you can make all the columns wider or smaller by dragging the tab (two tiny vertical lines) at the bottom of the divider bar that separates the columns. However, if you want to adjust the width of just one column (while leaving the other columns untouched), hold the Option key before you drag the column divider bar.

JUMPING FROM COLUMN TO COLUMN

When you're in Column View, you can jump from column to column by pressing the Option-Right Arrow keys. If you want to jump backward (to the previous column), use Option-Left Arrow.

OPENING FOLDERS IN NEW WINDOWS

Personally, I really like the way some things worked back in Mac OS 9. In particular, I liked that when I opened a new folder, a new window opened with the contents of that folder. As you've probably noticed, by default Mac OS X doesn't do that: if you double-click on a folder, that folder's contents are revealed in your current window. Well, if you're like me, you'd like these folders to open in their own separate window (as in previous versions of the Mac OS). So go under the Finder menu, under Preferences, and choose "Always open folders in a new window." Ahhh, that's better!

   NEW WINDOWS FOR FOLDERS, PART 2

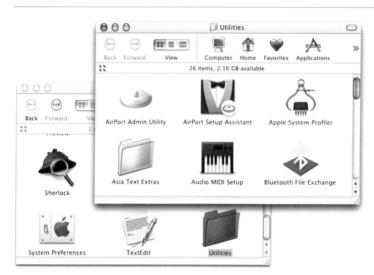

If you want to make use of Mac OS X's "everything opens in the same window" scheme, but occasionally you want to open a folder in its own separate window, just hold the Command key then double-click on the folder.

   IN LOVE WITH COLUMN VIEW? MAKE IT A PERMANENT THING

Since Icon View and List View have been around for over a decade, it's not surprising that many longtime Mac users absolutely fall head-over-heals in love with Mac OS X's lovely new Column View. If you're one of those lovelorn users, you can request that all new windows automatically open in Column View. Just go under the Finder menu, under Preferences, and click on the checkbox for "Open new windows in Column View." This turns every new window into a moment of unbridled passion that knows no bounds. Well, it does for some people anyway.

SHOW ME THE WAY TO GO HOME

Since nearly all of your individual files, with the exception of your applications, will live in your Home folder, there's a keyboard shortcut you should become familiar with right away. It's Shift-Command-H, and pressing it while in the Finder will bring your Home window front and center in a hurry. If speed isn't an issue (and when is speed *not* an issue?) you can also click on the Home icon in the Toolbar (if you have the Toolbar visible).

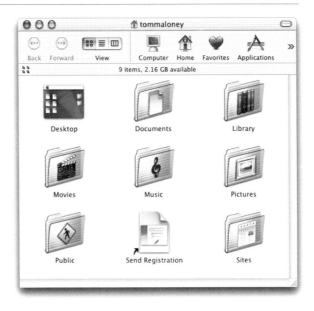

   WANT FOLDERS TO OPEN IN NEW WINDOWS? HIDE THE TOOLBAR!

If you're working in a window while in Icon or List View and you want any folders you open to open in their own separate window, just press Command-B first. This will hide the Toolbar, and by doing so, all folders that you double-click on will now open in their own window.

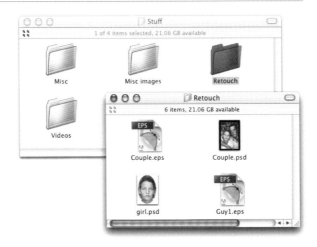

ONE-CLICK TRAIL TO YOUR FILE

This one's a handy holdover from Mac OS 9.x (and previous versions of the Mac OS). If you Command-click on a Window's title bar, a pop-up menu will appear that shows its folder hierarchy (which folders your current window resides within).

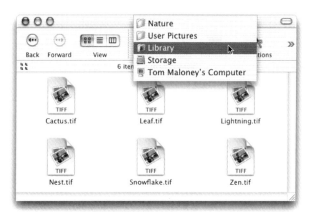

   ## HIDING THE TOOLBAR WHEN YOU DON'T NEED IT

If you don't want the Toolbar showing all the time (or ever for that matter), you can hide it by simply clicking on the pill-shaped icon on the top right of the window's title bar.

YOU CAN ALWAYS GO BACK

If you have the Toolbar hidden, with its all-important "Go Back" button, you can still go back to the previous window by pressing Command-[(that's the Left Bracket key, which appears diagonally to the left of the Return key on your keyboard).

AN ALTERNATIVE TO THE TOOLBAR

If you've hidden your Toolbar (and many well-bred people often do), you don't have to make it visible just to use its functions. Just look under the Go menu, and you'll find the default Toolbar items right there (like Home, Computer, Favorites, Applications), just waiting for you to mess with 'em.

   TOGGLING THE TOOLBAR

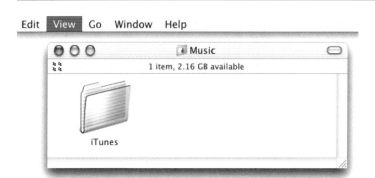

If you need to make a quick click in the Toolbar, but you like to keep it hidden, then just press Command-B to make it visible, and Command-B to hide it again.

   THE ULTIMATE CUSTOMIZE TOOLBAR SHORTCUT

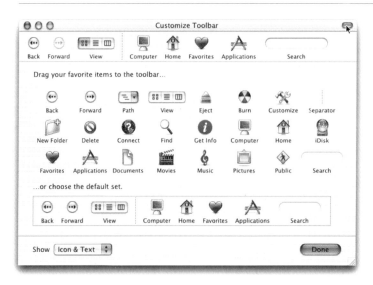

If you want to customize the items in your Toolbar (and there's nothing wrong with that), just Shift-click the little white pill-shaped button at the top right of your window's title bar, and the Customize Toolbar dialog will appear, right there in your window.

   MOVE YOUR TOOLBAR ICONS AT WILL

If you decide you want to change the order of the icons in your Toolbar, just hold the Command key and drag them where you want them.

  HOW TO MAKE THE TOOLBAR WORK LIKE THE DOCK

Earlier in this chapter, I showed how you can customize the Toolbar using the Customize Toolbar command. But you can add other icons to this window that make it even more powerful. For example, if you use Photoshop a lot, just open the window where your Photoshop application resides, drag the Photoshop icon right up to the Toolbar, and the other icons in the Toolbar will move out of the

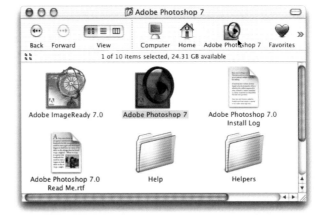

way. Now you can use this window Toolbar kind of like you would the Dock—you can even drag-and-drop images you want to open right onto the Photoshop icon.

   TOO MANY ICONS IN YOUR TOOLBAR? SHRINK 'EM

The Toolbar icons are fairly large, taking up considerable space both vertically and horizontally. If you add a few extra icons to the Toolbar, the additional icons could wind up being hidden from view. What can you do? Well, you can have the Toolbar display just the icons,

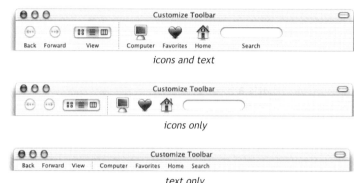

icons and text

icons only

text only

which saves space by removing the text and shrinking the space between the icons.

To display the Toolbar items by icon, rather than by icon and text, Control-click anywhere in the Toolbar and choose icons only. If you really want to shrink the Toolbar to its bare minimum, try Text Only.

   SEPARATING THE RIFF-RAFF IN YOUR TOOLBAR

I remember the first time I saw a Separator Bar in someone's Toolbar. I thought, "This is the slickest person in the world," or maybe it was "Gee, I wonder how they got that separator!" I can't remember which. Either way, they're handy and look cool. To get yours, just Shift-click on the little pill-shaped icon in the top right of your title bar to bring up the Customize Toolbar dialog box. Then, in the collection of icons that appears in the dialog, just drag the Separator icon and drop it right where you want it in the

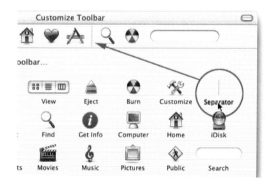

Toolbar. I use the Separator Bar as a visual separator between all my apps/folders and the Trash icon that lives in my Toolbar. But hey, that's just me.

WHAT ARE THOSE TWO LITTLE GRAY ARROWS IN MY TOOLBAR?

If you've added a number of icons to your Toolbar and suddenly they're not there, either of two things has happened: (1) you accidentally reinstalled Mac OS X off the original install disks (that's a joke—no one "accidentally" installs an OS. Well, it's at least very rare). Or (2) what's probably happened is that you've shrunken the size of your window, and when you do that, Mac OS X automatically hides the extra Toolbar icons and replaces them with those two little gray arrows.

Luckily, they're "clickable," so just click on them and a pop-up menu will appear giving you access to any hidden Toolbar icons. When you expand the window back out, the icons reappear and the little gray arrows go away.

NAMING TOOLBAR ITEMS TRICK

For some reason, Mac OS X won't let you rename any of your icons once they're in the Toolbar, so if you want them to have different names, you'll have to either (a) rename them before you drag them up to the Toolbar, or (b) create an alias of each item, give the alias the name you want, then drag their icons up to the Toolbar.

  GETTING BACK YOUR TOOLBAR DEFAULTS

If you've made a total mess of your Toolbar, there's no button for returning the icons to the default set, but getting them back there is fairly easy. First, Shift-click on the white pill-shaped button at the top right of your window's title bar to bring up the Customize Toolbar dialog. In the bottom left of the Customize Toolbar dialog, you'll see a set called "the default set." Drag it up top and it will replace the current icons in your Toolbar.

   SPEED TIP: REMOVING TOOLBAR ICONS

To remove an icon from the Toolbar, you don't have to go digging through the View menu to get the Customize Toolbar dialog. Instead, just hold the Command key, click on the icon, and simply drag it off the Toolbar.

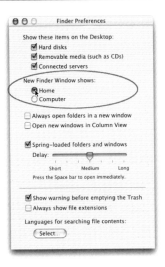

THE BAD KEYBOARD SHORTCUT HALL OF FAME: NEW FOLDERS

For about 16 years the keyboard shortcut for creating a New Folder on a Macintosh was Command-N (and it made perfect sense, because we make so many new folders). Apparently, it was too perfect, because in Mac OS X Apple changed it. Now it's Shift-Command-N. Of all the changes in Mac OS X, this one really just doesn't make any sense to me. If you forget, and press the old Command-N, you get a new Finder window, which I find about as useful as fish might find a bicycle. If you want to make the Shift-Command-N keyboard shortcut at least marginally helpful, go under Finder and choose Finder Preferences. In the Finder Prefs dialog, for "New Folder Window shows" choose "Home" instead of Computer. At least that way, if you press it, it'll open your Home window, which you will use quite often.

SPEED TIP: CREATING NEW FOLDERS

Okay, so Apple took our beloved "Command-N creates a New Folder" keyboard shortcut from us, but that doesn't keep us from being one click away from a new folder. Just Shift-click on the little white pill-shaped button in the top right of a window's title bar to bring up the Customize Toolbar window. Drag the New Folder icon to your Toolbar, and then you're one click away from a New Folder any time you need one.

STOP THE SCROLLING BLUES

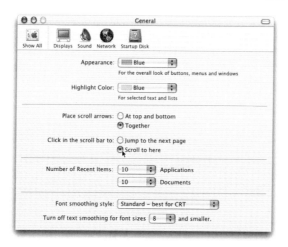

If you don't like sliding the scroll bar up and down in your documents, you can turn on a feature called "scroll to here" that lets you jump to any position in the scroll bar by just clicking on it (rather than using the scroll handles themselves). To turn this on, go under the Apple menu, under System Preferences, and click on the General icon. When the General Preferences pane appears, for the setting called "Click in the scroll bar to," choose "Scroll to here."

ANOTHER ANTI-SCROLL BAR TIP

Speaking of hating to use the scroll bars, you can always use the Page Up/Page Down keys on your keyboard to move up and down. Hey, think of it this way—your hands are already resting on the keyboard—now you don't have to grab the mouse at all. (Note: If you have a PowerBook, hold the "fn" key and then press the Up Arrow key for "Page Up" and the Down Arrow key for "Page Down.")

LABELS ARE GONE, SO TRY COMMENTS INSTEAD

In Mac OS X Apple did away with Labels (the ability to color-code icons and folders), but it replaced them with something many people like better—the ability to add a comment, which is visible in Finder windows set to List View. To add a comment (your personal note) to a file, just click on the file you want to add a comment to, and then press Command-I. The Info window will appear. Click on the right-facing gray triangle to the left of the word Comments to reveal a field for entering your personal notes. Just click in this field and start typing. When you're done, close the window. To see your comments when in List View, you first have to change a preference setting to make the Comments column visible. Make sure you're viewing your window in List View, and then press Command-J to bring up the View Options window. In the section called "Show columns," turn the checkbox on for "Comments." If you want every window in List View to show comments (not just the currently active window), make sure you check the "All windows" button at the top of the dialog.

   GETTING RID OF THE PREVIEW COLUMN

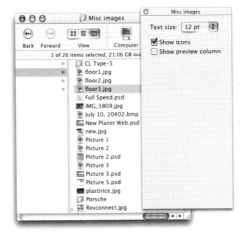

If you've used Mac OS X's Column View, you know that when you click on a file, you'll get a large preview of that file in a new column type called "The Preview Column." Click on a graphic—you see its preview. Large! This "feature" annoys the heck out of some people (you know who you are), so to turn off this special column, just view a window in Column View, then press Command-J to bring up the Column View Options. Turn off the checkbox for "Show Preview column" and this wonderful (yet occasionally annoying) preview column will disappear.

THE BUTTONS THAT LOOK LIKE HEADERS

By default, when you open a new window in List View, the files in that window are sorted alphabetically by name (makes sense, right?). However, if you decide that you'd like them sorted by Date Modified, Size, Kind, etc., just click on the appropriate header right under your Toolbar. Sure, they look like

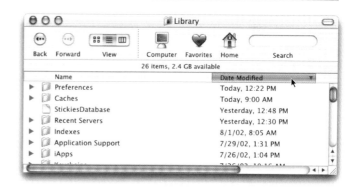

they're only headers, but in reality they're buttons. Click on one, and your window is now sorted by that criterion. If you want them sorted in reverse order (in other words, if you were sorting by size and you want the smallest file listed first, rather than the largest), then just click on the Arrow icon to the far right of the button's name.

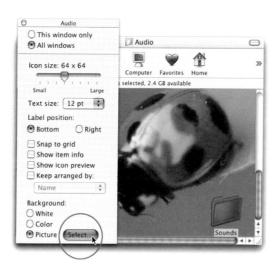 ## ADDING A PHOTO AS YOUR WINDOW'S BACKGROUND

As long as your Finder window is in Icon View, you can add a photo as its background. You do this by going under the View menu, under Show View Options, and in the Background section (at the bottom of the dialog box) choose Picture. Click on the Select button and the standard Open/Save dialog box will appear where you can choose which image you'd like to appear as the background of your window. Click OK and that image will then appear. Note: This works *only* when viewing the window in Icon View. If you change to List View, the image will no longer be visible.

SPEED TIP: NAVIGATING WITHOUT THE MOUSE

If you're looking for a faster way to navigate within Finder windows while you're in Icon View, try navigating using just your keyboard. Just as in previous versions of the Mac OS, you can use the Arrow keys on your keyboard to move from icon to icon, but you can also look inside folders by holding Command-Option and pressing the Down Arrow key. To go back up a level (i.e., close the folder and return to where you were), press Command-Option-Up Arrow.

 OLD WINDOW TIPS DIE HARD

Just as in previous versions of the Mac OS, if you're in a Finder window and type in the first letter of the name of the file you want—it will jump to that file (well, if that's the only file that starts with that letter. If there is more than one file with the same first letter, try typing the first two letters). This works in both Icon View and List View, but doesn't work in Column View. Also, once you've selected a file, if it's not the one you want, you can jump to the next file (alphabetically) by pressing the Tab key.

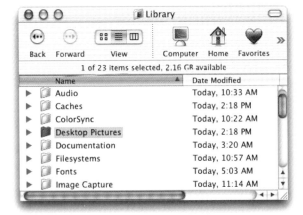

BEATING THE ALPHABETICAL TRAP

Want a particular file to appear at the top of your list when sorting in List View by name? Just type a blank space in front of its name, and it will jump to the top of the list. Extra tip: Don't forget that you've done this, or you'll always wonder why "whale photo" appears before "accounting report" when you're sorting alphabetically.

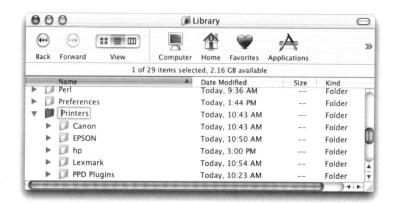

REARRANGING THE HEADERS IN LIST VIEW

Okay, let's say you're in List View and you decide that you want the Comments column to appear right after the Name column. You can make it so. Just click directly on the header named Comments and drag it horizontally along the bar until it appears right after Name. You can do the same with the other headers—move 'em where you want 'em. There's only one you can't move—the Name header. It's stuck in the first position.

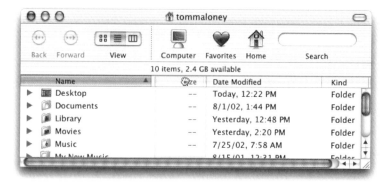

 RESIZING COLUMNS IN COLUMN VIEW

If you're using Mac OS X's handy Column View, you'll probably find many occasions where you wish one or more columns were wider. You can adjust the width of these columns by clicking-and-dragging on the two little lines that appear at the bottom of the divider line between columns. As you drag to the right, the width of all columns increases, and as you drag to the left (big surprise) they decrease.

 QUICKLY TOGGLE BETWEEN WINDOW VIEWS

You can quickly toggle between the three window views (Icon, List, or Column) by pressing Command-1, Command-2, and Command-3, respectively (which means, press them with respect).

CLOSING MULTIPLE WINDOWS

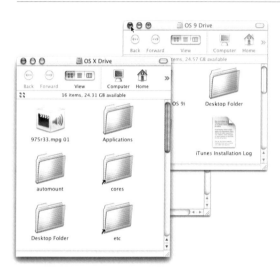

You can close all your open desktop windows by either Option-clicking on any window's close button, or pressing Option-Command-W.

   COOL WAYS TO MINIMIZE WINDOWS

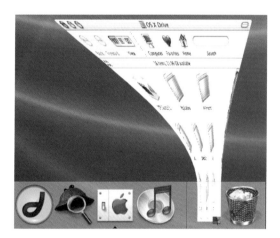

My favorite way to minimize a window down to the Dock is to just double-click on its title bar. Even better, if you want to minimize a "whole mess" of open windows (read as: all your open windows), Option-double-click on any title bar. If you don't care about these cool double-clicking shortcuts, you can just press Command-M to minimize the current window, but it's just so, so...trite.

WINDOW HOUSEKEEPING TIPS

If it looks as if someone tossed a grenade into your Finder window, scattering your icons everywhere with seemingly no rhyme or reason, then you need an icon housekeeper. The first time you do it, it's a quick two-step process, but from there on out your windows almost straighten themselves. First, make sure your window is in Icon View, and then go under the View menu, and choose Arrange by Name. This puts your icons neatly into rows, alphabetically from left to right, top to bottom. Next, press Command-J to bring up the View Options window. Choose "Snap to grid," and even if you move an icon, it will snap to an invisible grid to help keep things arranged and organized as your work. Ahh, isn't that better?

  SAVE TIME WHEN CHANGING VIEWS OF MULTIPLE WINDOWS

Back in previous versions of the Mac OS, every time you wanted to adjust the View Options for a window, you had to open the View Options dialog. So, if you wanted to adjust 10 windows, you had to open and close View Options 10 times. It was mind-numbing. Now, in Mac OS X, you can leave the View Options dialog box open the whole time, and adjust as many windows as you want. You can click on the window whose settings you want to see in the View Options, make your changes, close that Finder window, then click on the next window and make changes there—all without ever closing the View Options window. The View Options window always stays in front.

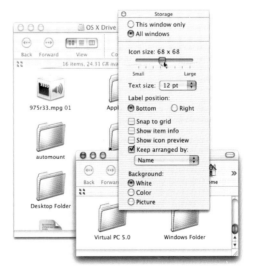

   THE WINDOW NAVIGATION TOOL BORROWED FROM PHOTOSHOP

If you use Photoshop (I've used it a couple times—it seems pretty nice), you're probably familiar with one of its tools called the Hand tool that lets you move the image around by clicking-and-dragging within in the image itself. Well, believe it or not, Mac OS X has a very similar tool. While in Icon or List View, just hold Option-Command and click within an

open space in your window and you can move up/down and left/right in any window that has scroll bars. Freaky, ain't it?

   THE JOY OF SPRING-LOADED FOLDERS

There was a Mac OS 9 feature called "Spring-loaded folders" that longtime Mac users liked pretty well. That is until Apple left it out of Mac OS X, and then it was as if Spring-loaded folders were the most critical single feature ever (in other words—we took it for granted, until it was gone). Luckily, in Jaguar it's made its triumphant return, and it works better than ever. It's designed to let you quickly navigate down through a number of folders, without having to waste time opening them one by one. Here's how to use it: Just drag an icon over a folder, hold it there for a moment, and the folder will automatically pop open revealing its contents. If there's another folder inside that folder, hold it over that one and it too pops open. If you change your mind, just move your icon out of the window, and all the folders automatically close themselves in a hurry. You can control the amount of time (from a short to a long delay) that it takes for a folder to "spring open" by going under the Finder menu and choosing Finder Preferences (you can also turn this feature off if it bothers you). If you're not sure how much delay you should choose, try Medium, and if you want a particular folder to spring open quicker, just press the Spacebar while your icon is hovering over the folder, and it will open immediately.

A CLEANER-LOOKING COLUMN VIEW

When you're viewing a Finder window in Column View, you might find it looks cleaner (and less intimidating) if you turn off the tiny little icons that appear before each file's name in Column View. To do that, make sure you're viewing a window in Column View, then press Command-J to bring up the View Options. In the View Options palette, turn off the checkbox for "Show Icons" and the tiny little rascals will be hidden from view, leaving you with a cleaner, less cluttered Column View. The downside? With the icons turned off, it's not easy to tell a folder, from a hard drive, from a file, but it sure is a fun diversion on a boring day. (Actually, this probably should have been in the Mac OS X Pranks chapter.)

   ## HOW TO TELL IF 'SNAP TO GRID' IS TURNED ON

If you're wondering if you have "Snap to Grid" turned on for a particular window, just look in the left-hand corner of the window's Status Bar. If Snap to Grid is turned on for that particular window, you'll see a tiny light-gray grid icon in the status bar.

for those about to dock!

DOCKING TIPS

You have to hand it to Apple: *When it comes to application launching and switching, with Mac OS X's Dock they have created the Venus Di Milo*

For Those About to Dock!
docking miracles made easy

of application launchers and switchers. Okay, that just sounds weird. How about, "…the crème de la crème" of launchers and application switchers? Nah, too "Frasier and Niles." Maybe the adjective isn't the problem—maybe it's the "launcher and application switcher" part—it just doesn't sound sexy enough to describe all the really cool things the Dock lets you do (which we look at in this chapter). Okay, how about this, "…when it comes to doing it, the Dock totally rocks!" Nah, that sounds too "Eminem." Instead, perhaps we should look at the word "Dock" itself. It's clearly a derivative of the popular Latin phrase "One, two, three-o-clock, four-o-clock, Dock," which, if memory serves me correctly, is inscribed on the torch held high by Lady Liberty in New York Harbor (and Lady Liberty was presented to the United States by French Prime Minister Bill Haley, around five, six, seven o'clock).

INSTANT DOCK RESIZE

If you want to make the Dock larger or smaller, there's a slider in the Dock Preferences pane, but you don't have to use it. Ever. That's because you can simply put your cursor right over the divider line on the right side of the Dock (the one that separates your apps from your folders and Trash) and your cursor will change to a horizontal bar with two arrows: one facing up and one facing down. When it does that, just drag your cursor upward to make the Dock bigger and downward to shrink it.

QUITTING APPLICATIONS RIGHT FROM THE DOCK

If you want to quit one or more applications which are currently running, you don't have to make each application active and then choose Quit (that just takes too long). There's a much faster way—just Control-click on the Dock icon for any running application and choose Quit from the pop-up menu that appears.

FREAKY MOVIE DOCK TRICK

This is one of those "show off your Mac" tricks that really amaze people, but outside of that, I haven't found a real use for it. You start by opening a QuickTime Movie, then hit the play button and watch it for a second or two. Then click the yellow center button in the title bar to shrink the movie to the Dock (it appears down by the Trash). Here's the cool thing: You'll notice the movie continues to play even while in the Dock. You can even hear the audio! Only ants can really enjoy it at this size (in fact, ants love this effect because to them, they're seeing your movie on the "big screen"), but the naked human eye can see the movie too. I've also tested this by putting my clothes back on, and even when not naked, my human eye can still see it. How cool is that?

   LITTLE YELLOW BUTTON TOO SMALL? TRY THIS!

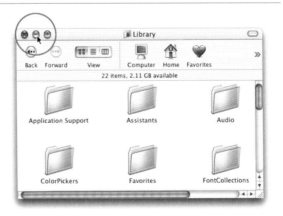

Sometimes hitting that tiny middle yellow button (to minimize your current window) is tricky, especially if you're using a Titanium PowerBook set at its native resolution, in which everything is smaller than a gnat's nose. If you'd like something bigger to aim at than that tiny yellow button, just double-click anywhere on the window's title bar and that window will immediately minimize to the Dock, just as if you clicked the tiny yellow button. Of course, you could skip the whole clicking thing altogether and just press Command-M, but that just seems like cheating now, doesn't it?

AUTOMATICALLY HIDING THE DOCK

The smaller your screen, the more important the ability to hide the Dock from view becomes (as you might imagine, this is a very popular feature for PowerBook users). Basically, with this feature active, the Dock hides off screen and only reappears when your cursor moves over the area where the Dock used to be. It kind of "pops up" so you can work in the Dock until you move away, and then it hides again. To turn this Dock feature on, go under the Apple menu, under Dock, and choose Turn Hiding On. If you think you might use this function often, you'll probably want to memorize the Turn Hiding On/Off shortcut, which is Option-Command-D.

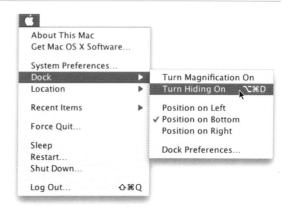

   FOR THOSE WHO DON'T WANT TO "HIDE"

If the Dock seems to be in your way a lot, but you don't like the whole "hiding the Dock" thing, try setting the dock to its smallest size (so you can barely notice it's there at all). Then, turn on Magnification and set it to a pretty large size, so when you scroll your mouse over the tiny Dock, the icons jump up in size so you can see what's what. You can turn Magnification on by going under the Apple menu, under Dock, and choosing "Turn Magnification On."

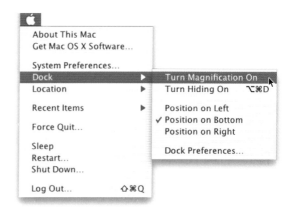

TOO LAZY FOR A TRIP TO THE DOCK?

If you don't feel like moving your cursor all the way down to the Dock to change applications, you can easily rotate the open applications to front by pressing Command-Tab.
Each time you press it, the next application in the Dock moves to front. Want to
cruise through the icons in your Dock in reverse (from right to left)? Just press
Shift-Command-Tab. Hey, somebody might want to do this. Really.

EJECT DISKS FROM THE DOCK

Want to eject a Zip disk, CD, or
FireWire drive from your desktop? Just
drag it to the Trash icon in your Dock,
and as you approach the Dock, you'll
see the Trash icon change into an
Eject button. When you drop your
drive's/CD's/disk's icon on the Eject

button, only one thing can happen—it erases the contents of your disk. Kidding! Just a
joke. Actually, of course, it ejects your disk/CD/drive.

GET RIGHT TO THE FILE YOU WANT

If you've parked a folder full of files in the Dock, you don't have to open the folder to get to a particular file. Instead, just Control-click on the folder. A pop-up list of all the files in that folder will appear, and you can go right to the file you want to open from this pop-up menu.

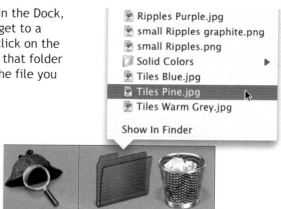

   FOLDERS TO ADD TO YOUR DOCK

Adding folders to your Dock can be a real timesaver, and two of the most popular folders to add to the Dock are your Home folder and your Applications folder. Another thing you might consider, rather than putting your entire applications folder on your Dock, is to create a new folder and put in it aliases of just the applications and system add-ons (such as the Calculator, etc.) that you really use. Then you can access these by Control-clicking on the folder in the Dock, and a pop-up list will appear that looks a lot like the Apple menu from OS 9.

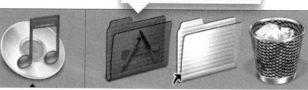

KEEPING A RUNNING APP IN THE DOCK AFTER YOU QUIT

If you're running an application and you say to yourself, "You know, I use this app a lot," you can keep its icon in the Dock, even after you've quit the app, so next time it's just one click way. Just Control-click on the app's icon in the Dock, and choose "Keep in Dock." Of course, there is another way. A cooler way. An "I don't need no stinkin' pop-up menu" way. Just click on the running application's icon, drag it away from the Dock, pause a second, and then drag it right back. It's really no faster, but it makes you look (and feel) less pop-up menu co-dependent.

 UNLOADING THE DOCK

If you have a few apps running and you like to keep things uncluttered and organized by minimizing document windows to the Dock, it doesn't take long before your Dock gets pretty crowded. If that's the case, here's a tip that might help you bring some welcome space, and order, back to your Dock: When you're switching from one application to the next, hold the Option key before you click on the new application's icon in the Dock. This hides all of the Dock icons for minimized windows from the application you just left, and helps unclutter the Dock. When you switch back to that application later, its minimized windows reappear in the Dock.

WHY SOME ICONS WON'T LEAVE THE DOCK

There are a couple of icons that live in the Dock, and Apple thinks that's exactly where they belong, so they won't let you pull them out of the Dock. Apple figures you're always going to need the Finder, you need the Trash too, and they won't let you remove the icon of any application

that is currently running (after all, if they did let you remove the icon, how would you get back to the application? It would just run forever, kind of like a Flying Dutchman). So in short, don't waste your time trying to drag those puppies from the Dock—they're stuck there (for your protection).

   UNDOCKING AN APPLICATION WHILE IT'S RUNNING

If you're running an application that you normally keep in the Dock, but you decide that you really don't want it to live in the Dock any longer, you don't have to quit before removing it—just drag the icon off the bar while it's still running. Don't let it freak you out that the application icon still appears in the Dock (it has to, by Federal law). But when you do finally quit the application, take a look in the Dock, and the icon is now removed permanently (by permanently, I mean until you stick it back there again when you realize that you use that application more than you thought).

JUMP RIGHT TO THE FINDER WINDOW YOU WANT

If you're working in an application, and you want to go to the Finder (desktop), you have to click on the Finder icon in the Dock, right? Well, there's a way you can save time by jumping directly to any open window in the Finder. That's right, just Control-click on the Finder icon in the Dock, and a pop-up list of open Finder windows will appear where you can select the window you want to jump to.

   ## DON'T JUST JUMP TO FINDER WINDOWS...

In the above tip, I mentioned you could jump to any open Finder window by Control-clicking on the Finder icon? Well, that doesn't just hold true for the Finder; you can pull off a similar stunt with applications and jump directly to any open document within a running application. Just Control-click on the application's icon in the Dock, and then in the pop-up menu choose the document name you want to jump to.

CHAPTER 2 • Docking Miracles Made Easy   **39**

BRING AN APP TO FRONT

If you have multiple applications open (oh, and you will), you'll find yourself switching between applications quite often. To bring an application to the front and hide the previous application you were using, just Option-click on the application's icon in the Dock.

FIND A DOC'S HOME RIGHT FROM THE DOCK

If you have a folder full of documents in the Dock, here's a shortcut to get Mac OS X to open the document's Finder window rather than opening the document itself. First, Control-click on the folder to bring up a list of the folder's contents, and then Command-click on the file you want to find on your drive.

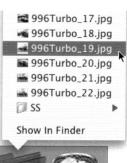

BRINGING HOME LOST SHEEP: FINDING DOCKED ORIGINALS

Okay, so you see the application's (or document's) icon in the Dock, but you have no earthly idea where the app (or doc) really resides on your hard drive. It's there somewhere, but you really don't know where, and that scares you (well, it scares me anyway). To find where the docked application or document really lives, just Control-click on it in the Dock and choose "Show in Finder." The window where it lives will immediately appear on screen.

   STOP THE BOUNCING. I BEG YOU!

When you launch an application, it begins to bounce incessantly in the Dock, in a distracting vertical Tigger-like motion, until the app is just about open. I love this feature; but then, I enjoy having my cavities drilled. If you enjoy this animation as much as I do, you can turn it off by going to the Apple menu, under Dock, and choosing Dock Preferences. When the Dock Preferences pane appears, turn off the checkbox (it's on by default) for "Animate opening applications." Turning this off now can save you thousands in therapy costs down the road.

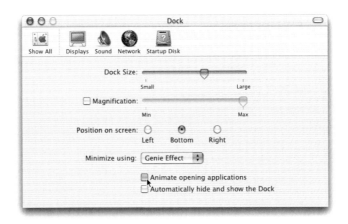

FREAKY GENIE EFFECT

There's a little trick you can pull to make the Genie Effect (the little animation that takes place when you minimize a window to the Dock) even freakier (we call it the freaky genie). Just hold Shift before you minimize the window and it puts the Genie effect into a "super slo-mo" mode that looks kinda cool. I say "kinda" because this effect (like the Genie Effect itself) gets old kinda quick, but people who've never seen it before dig it. At least at first.

   MAKE ONE ACTIVE, AND HIDE THE REST

If you want to make just the application you're working on visible, and hide all the other running applications, including any open Finder windows, just hold Option-Command, and then click on the application's icon in the Dock. This is much faster than choosing your application, then going under your application's menu and choosing "Hide Others."

Adobe Photoshop 7

THE NON-CLOSING SYSTEM PREFERENCES

Have you noticed that if you open the System Preferences, make your adjustments, and then close the System Preferences window, its Dock icon still shows it's running? That's because it is. Even though the System Preferences window isn't open, just closing the window doesn't quit the System Preferences. You actually have to click on the icon to bring it to the front again and press Command-Q to quit the preferences and remove the System Prefs icon from the Dock. Weird. I know.

 ## FORCE QUITTING WITHOUT BRINGING DOWN YOUR MAC

If you're running an application in Mac OS X and for some reason it locks up or crashes (hey, it happens—remember, Apple didn't say applications wouldn't crash in Mac OS X; it said if they did, it doesn't bring down your whole system), you can easily Force Quit the application by Control-clicking on its icon in the Dock, and a pop-up menu will appear. Press the Option key, and you'll see the menu item called "Quit" change to "Force Quit." Click that, and it will force quit the application. Also, if you're a longtime Mac user, you might be afraid to Force Quit an application, because back in Mac OS 9 (and prior to that) force quitting was an absolute last resort in hopes of saving an open document. If you were lucky enough to get Force Quit to work without locking up the machine (believe me—it was luck—force quitting in Mac OS 9 and earlier usually brought the whole machine down), then all you could really do was restart anyway, but at least you got to save your document. Mac OS X is designed to let you force quit then continue to work, so don't be hesitant to use this feature.

OPEN DOCUMENTS WITH THE DOCK'S DRAG-AND-DROP FEATURE

Remember how back in Mac OS 9, if you tore the Application menu off and had it floating around your desktop, you could drag-and-

drop documents onto an application listed in the menu, and it would endeavor to open them? You can do the same thing now in Mac OS X with the Dock—just drag documents directly to an application icon on the Dock, and if it thinks it might be able to open the document, the icon will highlight, basically telling you "let 'er rip!"

    STOP THE ICONS FROM MOVING

In the tip above (drag-and-drop to the Dock) I showed how you can drag a document onto an application's icon in the Dock. But some-times you may be trying

to add the document to a folder in the Dock. When you do this, the Dock thinks you're actually trying to add the document to the Dock itself, rather than dropping it on the folder, so it kindly slides the icons out of the way to make room for your document. That's incredibly polite (for an operating system anyway), but it can also be incredibly annoying if that's not what you're trying to do. If this happens to you, just hold the Command key as you drag and the icons will stay put, enabling you to drop the document into a "non-moving" object.

   DRAG-AND-DROP TO THE APP OF YOUR CHOICE

You can use the Dock to open a document in the application of your choice rather than what OS X would open it in normally by default. For example, let's say you make a screen capture using the

standard Shift-Command-3 shortcut, and the resulting PDF file then appears on your desktop. If you double-click that file, by default it's going to open in Preview, Mac OS X's app for viewing graphics. But what if you want it to open in Photoshop instead? Well, as long as Photoshop is in your Dock, you can drag the PDF screen capture from your desktop and drop it directly on the Photoshop icon in the Dock, and then Photoshop will open the document.

   FORCING A DOCUMENT ON AN APP

Sometimes, docked apps don't want to open your document, even though they may be able to, so you have to coax (okay, force) them to give it a

try. For example, let's say you created a document in WordPerfect for Mac a few years back. If you drag that document to Microsoft Word's icon in the Dock, chances are it won't highlight (which would be the indication it can open that document). If that happens, just hold Option-Command, then drag the icon to the Word icon in the Dock, and you can force it to try to open that document.

DOCK PREFERENCES SHORTCUT

You don't always have to go digging through the System Preferences just to make a quick change to the Dock's preferences. I guess Apple figured you'd be messing with them enough that they included the most popular Dock prefs right under the Apple menu, under Dock. If the preference you want isn't there, it's not a wasted trip because the last item in the Dock menu is Dock Preferences. Choose it, and the full Preferences pane appears.

 EVEN FASTER THAN THE DOCK PREFERENCES SHORTCUT

You learned above a quick way to get to the Dock's preferences, but now I think you're ready for the absolute fastest way there is to access the Dock prefs. This tip is so shrouded in Dock secrecy, I don't think even Apple knows it exists (of course they do, but I doubt they'd admit it without administering some sort of "truth serum.") Just Control-click on the divider line on the right side of the Dock and a pop-up list of Dock preferences is right there, just one click away.

SNAPPING DOCK SIZES

In a previous tip, I showed how you can resize the Dock by clicking on the divider line, but if you hold the Option key first and then start dragging, the Dock will "snap" to some preset sizes. Who chose these preset sizes? Probably Apple's software engineers, but some feel the presets were secretly designated by high-ranking government officials in yet another attempt to exert more "big brother-like" control over our otherwise mundane lives. Personally, I tend to think it was Apple, but hey, that's just me.

MINIMIZING MULTIPLE WINDOWS AT ONCE

If you have three or four open windows and want to minimize them all to the Dock at once, just hold the Option key and double-click on the title bar of any one of them, and all open windows will go to the Dock. Be careful when you do this, because if you have 50 open windows, they're all headed to the Dock in a hurry, and there's no real undo for this. Worse yet, you'll eventually have to pull 50 very tiny icons from the Dock one by one. So—make sure that's really what you want to do before you Option-double-click.

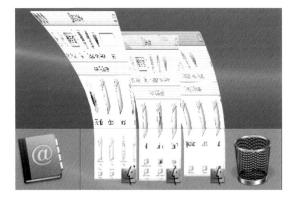

   FULL-SPEED DOCKING

The "Genie Effect" that occurs when you send a document to the Dock sure looks cool, but things that look cool generally eat up processing power, and that holds true with the Genie Effect as well. Turn off the Genie Effect and use the "Scale Effect" by going to the Dock Preferences (under Dock in the Apple menu) and choosing Scale Effect from the "Minimize using" pop-up menu at the bottom of the

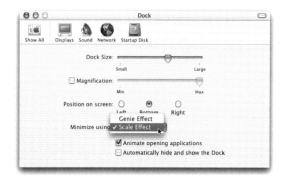

pane. (Check out Chapter 5 to find out "how to make annoying things go away" for this and other similar tips.) This decreases the burden on the system resources and keeps things moving at full speed.

Now, you might be tempted to skip this chapter if you think it's just about copying an icon from one file to another (it includes that, of

Icon See Clearly Now

sorry...not funny

course, but it's really much, much more). You might also be tempted to skip this chapter because you're upset that I couldn't come up with a chapter title using a decent song title, movie title, or popular band name that uses the word "icon." Leaving me no choice but to hack up the name of the 1972 hit by Johnny Nash "I Can See Clearly Now," in a desperate moment I wish I could take back. You might skip this chapter if you're the kind of person that just indiscriminately skips chapters, or perhaps you might skip this chapter as a personal form of protest because you believe, like many others, that icons are really part of a much broader government conspiracy to control our lives and eventually take away our right to bear arms. Ahhh, that's what it is. I knew if I kept digging, I'd uncover the real reason. Now, tell me about your mother…

ICON SUPERSIZING TIP

They're your icons; choose your favorite size. You can control the size that your icons appear when viewing a window in Icon View by pressing Command-J, which brings up the View Options dialog. You'll find a slider in there where you can size your icons to your heart's content, and there's a pop-up menu for choosing the Text size as well. You can also choose whether this icon size is just for the current window, or make it across the board in every window, by choosing "All windows."

GETTING TO THE GOODIES FAST

Want fast access to the most commonly used icon-related tasks? Just Control-click directly on an icon and a pop-up menu will appear with a list of tasks you're likely to take advantage of at one time or another.

DON'T LIKE THE ICON? USE A DIFFERENT ONE

Just as in previous versions of the Mac OS, if you don't like a file's icon, you can change it. (Check out www.iconfactory.com or www.xicon.macnn.com. They both have a fantastic selection of photo-quality Mac OS X icons ready to download.) To copy an icon from one file to another, just click on the icon you want to copy and press Command-I to bring up its Info window. When it appears, just press Command-C and it will automatically copy that file's icon to the Clipboard. Then go to the file whose icon you'd like to replace, press Command-I to bring up its Info window, then just press Command-V to paste the new icon into place. That's it! Piece of cake. Can of corn. Etc.

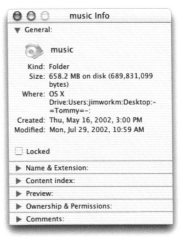

DON'T LIKE YOUR SHINY NEW CUSTOM ICON?

If you've added a custom icon to one of your files, and later grow tired of it (custom icons sometimes do get old, just like songs on the radio. You love 'em the first time you hear them, but then after hearing it for about the 200th time, the song you once loved is now so...played), then just click on the icon, press Command-I, then press Command-X, and the file's original icon will pop back into place (no radio pun intended).

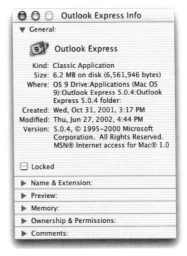

COPY AND DELETE AT THE SAME TIME

If you're archiving a file to disk (let's say to an external FireWire drive for example) you can drag the icon of the file you want to archive directly to that drive and the Mac will write a copy to that drive. However, your original file still lives on your current hard drive. If you want to have that file deleted from your drive as soon as it's copied to another drive, just hold the Command key as you

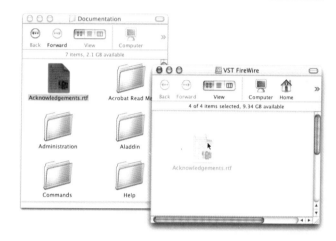

drag your icon, and the Mac will do two tasks for you—copy the file to the new drive, and delete the original from your drive.

   NEW FOLDER SPEED TIP

Need another folder to store your files and refuse to use the new keyboard shortcut Shift-Command-N? I don't blame you. Just Control-click on an empty space in any Finder window, and then choose New Folder from the pop-up menu.

CLEANING UP WINDOWS, ONE ICON AT A TIME

Want to bring some order back to your icons? Just hold the Command key while dragging any icon, and when you release the mouse button, it will automatically snap to an invisible alignment grid, helping, once again, to keep your icons tidy and organized. See, Mac OS X cares. Another way to "clean up" on an icon-by-icon basis is to click on the icon you want aligned, and then choose "Clean Up Selection" from the View menu.

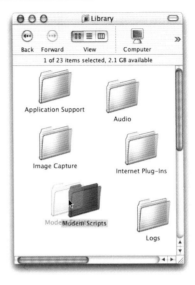

   ICON ORGANIZING TIPS

I cover these in more detail in the chapter on window tips, but I was afraid you might come here instead, looking for ways to organize your icons, so I'm going to quickly recap them in this one tip:

- To have your icons snap to an invisible alignment grid (to help keep them organized in rows) press Command-J and in the View Options dialog choose "Snap to grid."
- If you don't have "Snap to grid" on and you want a particular icon to snap to the grid, just hold the Command key while you drag the icon.
- To have your icons sorted alphabetically in rows, go under the View menu, click on "Keep arranged by," and then choose "Name" from the pop-up list.

DUPLICATING FILES THE FAST WAY

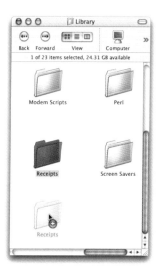

Want to copy a file? Piece of cake—in Icon or List View just hold the Option key, click on its icon, and drag yourself a copy. This makes an exact duplicate of the entire file, and it's even courteous enough to add the word "copy" to the end of the file name. How's that for service?

   CREATING ALIASES, AND THEN RECOGNIZING THEM LATER

To create an alias (a link to the actual file or application) just click on the icon and press Command-L (an easy way to remember this shortcut is to think of "L" for "Link.") The names of aliases are no longer italicized (thankfully), but their icons have a tiny little diagonal arrow in the lower-left corner to let you know they're aliases.

Mac OS X
KillerTips

  INSTANTLY FIND THE ORIGINAL FOR ANY ALIAS

Since an alias is just a copy of the file's icon (not the actual file itself), you may need to find the original at times. To do that, just click on the alias and press Command-R and the "Real" file will appear on screen in its window.

   CREATING ALIASES WITHOUT THE WORD "ALIAS"

Do you find it as annoying as I do that Mac OS X adds the word "alias" every time you create an alias? (I know, previous versions of the Mac OS did that as well, and it annoyed me there too.) Well, you can bypass the "adding-the-word-alias" uglies altogether by holding the Option and Command keys, and dragging the original file outside the Finder window it's currently in (I usually just drag mine to the desktop). This creates an alias without the word "alias" attached. (Note: Don't worry, you'll still know it's an alias, because its icon will have a tiny arrow at the bottom left-hand corner.)

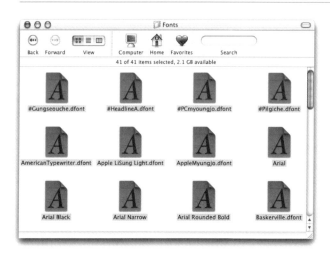 ## MOVING ALL THE ICONS AT ONCE

Want to select every icon in a window all at the same time? You don't? Then skip this tip. For everybody else, just press Command-A (Select All) and every icon in the window becomes highlighted, and you can now move them as a group.

 ## HOW TO SELECT ALMOST EVERYTHING

I've had dozens of occasions where I want to select "almost" everything in a window. For example, I want all the documents, but not any subfolders. If this happens to you (and it probably will), press Command-A to select everything in the window, then continue to hold the Command key and click only on the icons you *don't* want selected (like the folders in my example). This Command-clicking deselects them from the group.

DRAG-SELECTING MULTIPLE ICONS

If you want to select more than one icon at a time, just click-and-drag a selection marquee around them. Any icons that fall within its border will be selected. If for some reason you included an icon that you didn't want selected, just Command-click on it and it will deselect.

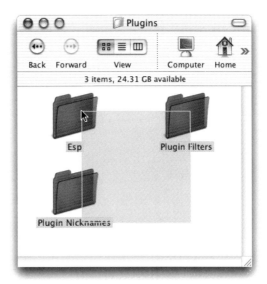

SELECTING MULTIPLE ICONS IN LIST VIEW

If you're in List or Column View and you want to select a series of icons, just click once on the top icon, hold the Shift key, and click on the last icon in the series that you want selected, and instantly, all the other icons between the first and last will be selected. Command-click to remove any selected icon that you want out of your "group."

SELECTING NONCONTIGUOUS ICONS IN LIST VIEW

If the headline for this tip doesn't sound both fun and fascinating, really, what does? It's really not as boring as it sounds. In List or Column View, to select more than one icon at a time that aren't contiguous, just hold the Command key and click on each icon. Click on any open space in the window or press Escape to deselect. In Icon view, you still Shift-click to add multiple icons to your selection.

   ## OPEN THE LONG FILENAME FLOODGATES!

The 31-character limit for naming files is *off,* and now you can create filenames up to 255 characters, as long as one of them isn't ":" (the Colon key, which is used by the system).

SUPER-FAST FILE RENAMING IN COLUMN VIEW

What's the quickest way to rename an icon while in Column view? In my opinion it's this: Select it, then press the Return key. The naming field becomes highlighted, then you can type in a new name. Press Return to lock in your change. If speed's not your game, and you would just prefer a nice wide-open field for renaming your icons, just click on the icon you want to rename. Then press Command-I to bring up its Info window. Then choose Name & Extension in the Info window, and you'll have an entire field to enter the name of your dreams.

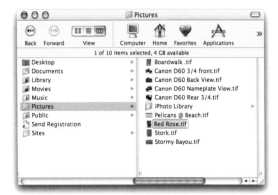

   NAMING SHORTCUTS

If you're naming a number of files with similar names (such as Fishing Trip 1, Fishing Trip 2, Fishing Trip 3, etc.), you can save time by highlighting the words "Fishing Trip" and pressing Command-C to copy those words to the Clipboard. Then, when you come to the next icon you want to rename, just press Return to highlight the name field, press Command-V to paste in the word "Fishing Trip," then press the Right Arrow key and enter the number for this file (like "4"), and so on. You can also copy and paste a name from

one folder to another, as long as these two identically named folders don't wind up in the same folder. That's a big no-no and you will be severely disciplined if that should happen (or at least a mean warning dialog will appear).

ADDING WORDS TO THE END OF FILENAMES

If you are in Icon or List View and you want to add to an existing file's name (for example, if you had a Photoshop file named "cruise collage" and you wanted to add the words "summer 2002" to the end), just click on the name directly below the icon to highlight the name, then press the Right Arrow key to jump to the end of the existing name. Then all you have to do is type in "summer 2002." Press the Return key to lock in your new name. Note: To add characters at the beginning of the name, do the same routine, just press the Left Arrow instead.

 DON'T START YOUR FILENAMES WITH...

You can use most any alpha or numeric characters when naming your files in the Save Sheet in Mac OS X; but it's just a little sticky about one particular character that it really doesn't want you to use in your file's name. Okay, it's more than a little sticky—it flat out won't let you do it. It's the ":" (colon) character. It also won't let you *start* a filename with a period (.)

/ from Guns & Roses

which it calls a "dot." You can use a period in the middle or end of your file name just not at the beginning. So that's the scoop—Mac OS X selfishly hogs the colon (that doesn't sound nice) and it won't let you start with a dot. Other than that—let 'er rip! However, according to Apple, there are some applications that won't let you use "/" (the Slash key) when naming a file. So I guess that leaves out naming a file "/from Guns & Roses." Pity.

MOVING ICON NAMES TO THE SIDE: IT'S UNNATURAL

You do *not* want to mess with this, because an icon's name is supposed to appear beneath the icon. It has been this way since the beginning of Mac-time, and moving the name so it appears to the right of the icon, rather than the time-honored tradition of appearing below it, is just plain sick. It's twisted, odd, and unnatural. It's not only weird and perverse, it's perverse and weird. Nevertheless, here's how to do it: Just open a window, click on the Icon View button, then press Command-J to bring up the View Options. Under Label Position choose Right, and the name of each icon will appear to the right of the icon (Yeech!). However, "Right is wrong!" Just so you know.

   ## GET PHOTO THUMBNAILS ON THE FLY

Tired of seeing the default icons for your digital photos? Then change just one tiny preference setting, and working with digital photos in Finder windows becomes infinitely easier. The Preference is called "Show Icon Preview" and turning it on automatically replaces the default file icons with thumbnail previews of your photos, so you can see what they look like right in the Finder window. This preview is only available when viewing a Finder window in Icon mode, so start by clicking on the View by Icon button in the Toolbar. Then press Command-J to bring up that window's View Preferences and turn on "Show icon preview." That's it—now your digital camera images won't have generic icons. Instead they'll display thumbnail photos of your full-sized images as their icons.

    SEE YOUR ICON'S HIDDEN INFO

If you want more info on your files than the standard Icon view will give (after all, it just gives you the file's name in Icon view), you might want to turn on "Show item info." This View Options setting adds an extra line of information below certain files and folders than can be very helpful. For example, with this preference turned on, not only do you get a folder's name, but just below the name (in unobtrusive light-blue, 9-pt. type) you'll see how many items are in that folder. If the file is a QuickTime movie (for example) the item info shows you the length of the movie. MP3 files show how long the song is. This also works on the desktop, where the item info appears in white with a black drop shadow. On the desktop, it shows the capacity of your hard disk, and how much space is still free. To turn this slick little feature on, just open the window (in Icon view of course) that you want to apply it to, then press Command-J to bring up its View Options. Then turn on the checkbox for "Show item info." If you want to show the item info for every window (globally), then choose the All Windows button at the top of the dialog.

show me
the way

NAVIGATION

TIPS

The title of this chapter, "Show Me the Way," is an obvious tribute to musician Peter Frampton. I feel that I owe him this tribute because one day

Show Me the Way
navigating your new world

I received an e-mail from a reader of one of my other books leading me to a Web site about Peter Frampton. On the site, Peter names his favorite movies, books, albums, etc., and among his favorite books he listed my book Photoshop Down & Dirty Tricks. *Of course, being a Frampton fan myself, I was really tickled, and learning this has changed my life in immeasurable ways. For example, if Peter Frampton (who is currently touring, by the way) is appearing in concert at any nearby venue, I can just drop by the box office, pay the admission price, and they'll give me a ticket to his upcoming performance. Not only that, but if I go to the local record store and try to buy any Peter Frampton CD (including his classic "Frampton Comes Alive" double-album set), they'll let me. No questions asked. All I have to present is my ID and credit card. How cool is that?*

SPEED TIP: TAKE OUT THE PAPERS AND THE TRASH

Want to empty the Trash without making a trip up to the Finder menu first? Then just Control-click on the Trash icon in the Dock and choose Empty Trash. Of course, you could also press Shift-Command-Delete, but

how much fun is that? Incidentally, if you want to get something into the Trash in a hurry, just click on it and press Command-Delete and that file will jump in the Trash lickety-split!

   HYPER-SPEED TRASH DUMPING

Is there a file on your drive that is so vile, so disgusting, and so plain bad that not only do you want it in the Trash but you want the Trash emptied the second it arrives there? Then boy do I have a keyboard shortcut for you. Click on the file that has a death wish and press Command-Delete, and then Shift-Command-Delete. Click OK and the deed is done.

SEE ALL YOUR FILE INFO AT ONCE

Although the Info window (where you get all the info on a selected file) has a fairly compact size (thanks to the use of collapsible info panels), you can also see all the info on a file at once—just click on each right-facing gray triangle, expanding each info panel to its full size and creating a tall "über Info window." Cool tip: Want to see these panels expand and collapse in slow motion? Just hold the Shift key as you click on the right-facing gray triangles.

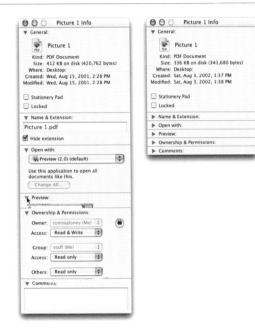

 LOOKING INSIDE MULTIPLE FOLDERS AT THE SAME TIME

Need to see what's inside more than one folder while in List View? Do it the fast way—Command-click on all the folders you want to expand, then press Command-Right Arrow. All the folders will expand at once. If the file you're looking for isn't there, just press Command-Left Arrow (you can do that, because your folders are still highlighted) to quickly collapse them all again.

BETTER THAN THE OLD CONTROL STRIP—IT'S MENU EXTRAS!

The Control Strip, thankfully, is gone and is replaced by something infinitely better—Menu Extras. These tiny black icons appear up in the Menu Bar, just to the left of your menu clock, and not only do they tell you what's going on, they actually work (at least if you click on them, anyway) kind of similar to how the Control Strip worked, but without the annoyance of the Control Strip (are you getting the feeling that I didn't like the Control Strip?). Just click on the Menu Extras to access their controls. For example, click on the one that looks like a speaker, and a volume control slider pops down, just like a menu, where you can control your system volume. You add Menu Extras in the System Preferences of each control you want to add. For example, you can add the Displays Menu Extra by going to the Displays Preference and choosing the "Show Displays in Menu Bar" checkbox.

 REARRANGE THE MENU EXTRAS

Want to change the order of the Menu Extras in your Menu Bar? Just hold the Command key and drag the icons into the order you want them. It gives you a real feeling of power. Well, a feeling of power over tiny icons anyway.

REMOVING MENU EXTRAS FROM YOUR MENU BAR

To remove a Menu Extra, just hold the Command key and click-and-drag the Extra right off the bar. It doesn't get much easier than that.

PLAYING FAVORITES

Do you find yourself going to the same folders over and over again? (Of course you do, we all do, we just don't admit it at parties.) Well if this sounds like you, it sounds as if folders that you go to again and again are your favorites, right? If so, click on one of these folders and press Command-T and then it's saved as a Favorite. That way, you can jump right to this "Favorites" folder from one of three handy places:

(1) Any Finder window Toolbar where Favorites is a default icon

(2) From the Go menu, under Favorites

(3) Perhaps more importantly, from any Open or Save Sheet

Note, if you realize that you're using a file or folder over and over again while you're in an Open or Save As Sheet, you'll find a button right in the Open/Save Sheet called "Add to Favorites" for adding that folder/file to your Favorites list.

DELETING FAVORITES

This is kind of weird but, as elegant and well-thought-out as *adding* a Favorite to Mac OS X is, it's kind of surprisingly clunky to *delete* a Favorite. Oh, it's easy, just clunkier than I thought it would be. You just open the Favorites folder by pressing Shift-Command-F. You'll see aliases to all your favorites within this folder. To delete one of these favorites, just drag it to the Trash. That's it. But it seems so... I dunno... unnecessarily manual.

   THE ACCIDENTAL DELETE PROTECTION DEVICE

In previous versions of the Mac OS, you could protect an important file from accidentally being deleted (trashed) by clicking on the "Locked" checkbox in the Info window. The problem was, you could still put the file in the trash, and if you held the Option key while emptying the trash, you could still delete it. Talk about a half-assed security device. Well, in Mac OS X, you apply the lock the same way (click on the file, press Command-I to bring up the Info window, and click on Locked), but the improvement comes in that Mac OS X will not even let you drag that file to the Trash in the first place. Instead, you get a warning dialog telling you basically, "Sorry punk." Hey, serves you right for trying to delete a file you thought was important.

DECIDED NOT TO SAVE AFTER ALL?

If you've opened the Save Sheet for a document (yup, it's called a "Sheet" now, rather than the Save As dialog box, because it's attached to your document and it pops down from the top of your document window...well, usually from the top. Occasionally, depending on the application, it appears from the side, but generally, it's from the top), and you decide that you don't want to save yet, you can press the Esc (Escape) key on your keyboard to cancel the process. You can also press the Cancel button, but that takes your hand off the keyboard.

   ## WHERE TO LOOK FOR YOUR FILES

By default, every time you save a document in Mac OS X, it assumes you're going to save it (okay, it secretly wants you to save it) in the Documents folder. So, if you're having trouble remembering where you saved a document, check the Documents folder first, because chances are it's there.

   SAVING TO THE DESKTOP IN A FLASH

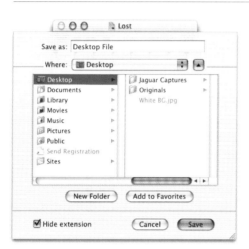

When you're in the Save As Sheet and you want to save a file to the desktop, just press Command-D and the "Where" pop-up menu will switch to Desktop, so all you have to do is name your file and click OK.

   BRINGING YOUR SAVED DOCUMENTS HOME

Okay, so you don't want to save your files to the Documents folder (like the OS really wants you to)? Then you probably want to save them to another folder inside your Home. When you're in the Save Sheet, press Shift-Command-H and Home will appear as your Save destination.

SAVING WHERE YOU WANT TO

When the Save Sheet appears, by default it appears in a "simple" mode, asking only what you want to name the file, and there's a simple pop-up menu for where you want to save it (and again, it assumes you want to save everything in the "Documents" folder). However, if you want (or need) to go digging through your drive to find (or create) a folder that isn't on the pop-up menu, just click on the small blue button with the down-facing arrow on it to expand the Save As Sheet to include a Column View of your hard drive.

THE SAVE SHEET KNOWS WHERE YOU'VE BEEN

When you're saving your file, chances are the location where you want to save it (if not the Documents folder) is one of your Favorites. If that's the case, you don't have to go navigating all over your drive to get there, because your Favorites appear by default in the "Where" pop-down menu (you'll see them just below the grayed-out words "Favorite Places"). Also for your convenience, the last few folders you saved documents into appear below the grayed-out words "Recent Places."

  RESIZE THOSE OPEN/SAVE SHEETS

The Open Dialogs and Save Sheets are totally resizable—just click on the bottom right-hand corner and start a-stretchin'.

   THE SAVE SHEET SAVES ITSELF

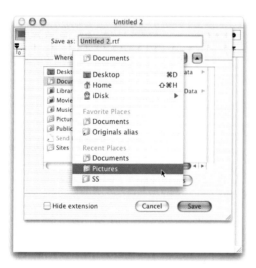

The Save Sheet has an excellent memory, because not only does it remember your Favorites and recent folders that you saved to but it also remembers if you expanded the Save Sheet into Column View or stretched out the size of the Save Sheet's dialog box. The next time you open that application and go to save a file, it will remember that you like the Column View and how large you made the dialog. It treats it as if you're setting "Save Sheet" defaults for that application.

AUTOMATICALLY ADD FILE EXTENSIONS

Sharing your files with someone using a PC? Make sure you name the file "Don't you wish you had a Mac.txt" or something like that (kidding). Actually, if you're sharing files with a PC, you can ask Mac OS X to automatically add the three-letter file extension to your files every time you save a file. Just go to the Finder Preferences and choose "Always show file extensions."

   ## HOW TO BE SELECTIVE WITH EXTENSIONS

In Mac OS X every file has a three-letter file extension (like PC files do) but by default, Mac OS X hides those three-letter extensions. In the previous tip, I showed you how to make those three-letter extensions visible all the time, but what if you just want to see the three-letter extensions for an individual file or two (kind of "once-in-a-while" visible file extensions)? If you want to see these extensions (perhaps if you're designing a Web graphic or two and want your files to have the .gif and .jpg file extensions visible), you can do that when you save each file. In the Save Sheet, you'll notice a checkbox called "Hide extension" which is on by

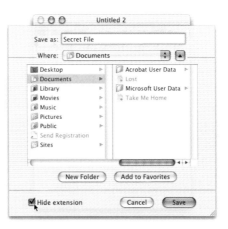

default. Just turn that checkbox off, and the appropriate file extension will be added to the file. In some applications, you may see a checkbox for "Append Extension" instead. In this case, make sure the checkbox is on to show the extension.

WHEN SAVING, ARE YOU STUCK WITH ONLY 31 CHARACTERS?

I Had A Bad Day because I grabbed what I thought was toothpaste, but it turned out to be|

Okay, you may be able to name a file in a Finder window with up to 255 characters, but can you do that in the standard Save As Sheet? Well, no. In most cases, you're still limited to the 31 characters from Mac OS days of old (I say in "most cases" because most of the software out there hasn't been updated to include a new Save As Sheet which will allow you to enter more than 31 characters). So, just save the file as "I had a bad day" within your Save As Sheet, but then switch to the Finder and add "because I grabbed what I thought was toothpaste, but it turned out to be..." while you're there.

SKIPPING THROUGH THE SAVE SHEET FIELDS

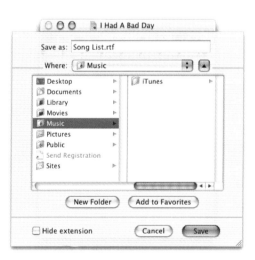

When you're in the Save Sheet and you've expanded to show the Column View, press the Tab key to jump from the Name field to the Column View field.

HOW MUCH SPACE DOES A DESKTOP TAKE?

How much space do the files sitting out there on your desktop take up? Believe it or not, you can find out. Just go to the desktop, make sure no icons are highlighted, then press Command-I to bring up the Info Window, and it will show you just how much space they're takin'. Why would you use this? I have no idea.

GIVING UP ON THE MOUSE AND DOIN' IT DOS-STYLE

Do you hate the mouse? I don't mean would you prefer to use a Wacom graphic tablet and wireless pen, I mean, "Do you hate using an external device, like a mouse, pen, etc. to control your Mac?" If so, perhaps you should use a PC, running DOS. Seriously, if that's the case (and it must be, for somebody somewhere), OS X does let you do just about everything from the keyboard, without any mouse involvement. You unleash this feature by pressing Control-F1 (which is the shortcut for turning on OS X's Full Keyboard Access), which lets you use the Control key, F-keys, and the Arrow keys on your keyboard to do just about everything you'd normally do

with a mouse. To see which keys do what, go under the Apple menu, under System Preferences, and click on the Keyboard icon. Then choose the Full Keyboard Access tab for all the gory details. Try it once, and you may never use the mouse again (I'm kidding. You will definitely use the mouse again—fairly soon I'd imagine).

 **FINDING SYSTEM PREFERENCES FAST BY SORTING ALPHABETICALLY**

If you've been using Mac OS X for a while, you've no doubt noticed that the System Preferences window puts all the individual preferences in horizontal rows, sorted by four categories (Personal, Hardware, Internet & Network, and System). That's great, if you know exactly which category to look under, but if you're new to Mac OS X, you might prefer a feature introduced in Jaguar—sorting the preferences alphabetically, rather than by category. That way, if you need the Universal Access preferences, you already know that alphabetically it's probably located near the end of the list. To sort your System Preferences alphabetically, first open the System Preferences window, then go under the View menu, and choose

Show All Alphabetically. If you later decide you'd like your categories back, just press Command-L while the System Preferences window is open.

   HIDING YOUR APPS SHORTCUT

This simple keyboard shortcut is one of my favorite Jaguar features. When you're at the Finder, you can hide all your running applications from view, by pressing Option-Command-H (the shortcut for Hide Others, which is found under the Finder menu). Ahhhhh, to me, that alone was worth the upgrade price (okay, it was almost worth the upgrade price).

FASTER CONTENT SEARCHES USING FIND

When you use Mac OS X's built-in Find function to search for content, by default it checks a number of different languages (besides English, it also searches Danish, Portuguese, Swedish, and half a dozen others). If you want to speed up your search, go under the Finder menu and choose Preferences. In the Finder Preferences dialog, click the Select button at the very bottom of the dialog under "Languages for searching file contents." In the dialog that appears, turn off the languages that you don't need searched, and it will make the indexing of your drive faster, and help "Find" find your stuff even faster.

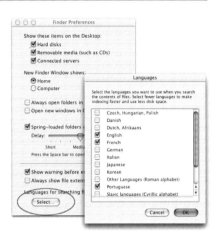

   A FASTER WAY TO GET YOUR SYSTEM INFO

If for some reason you run into some serious problems with your Mac (hey, it could happen), you might have to tell Apple tech support, a repair tech, or a Macintosh consultant some technical information about your particular hardware and system software configurations. Luckily, all that information is found by launching Apple's System Profiler. The only bad news is—it's buried deep within your Applications folder, inside your Utilities folder. Here's the tip: There's a quicker way to get to the Apple System Profiler. Just go under the Apple menu and choose About This Mac. When the dialog box appears, click on the button at the bottom called "More Info" and it will launch the Apple System Profiler for you right from there.

Mac OS X is an amazing operating system. Yet, it can also be an annoying operating system. So, depending on what you're doing with it—

She Drives Me Crazy

how to stop annoying things

it's either annoyingly amazing, or amazingly annoying. Okay, I'm not really being fair, because in reality, it's not the operating system itself that's annoying. It's things in the operating system—aspects of it (if you will) that are annoying. And not just a little annoying—we're talking "put you in a tower with a high-powered rifle and night-vision goggles" type annoying, and this chapter is how to quickly make some of the most egregious annoyances go away. But make no mistake about it— Mac OS X isn't the first Apple operating system to include wildly annoying features. Remember "Balloon Help?" Apple's attempt at coming up with a better form of onscreen help, which could have been devised only by the Prince of Darkness himself (not Darth Vader—El Diablo!)? There's a hint, just a hint, of that type of stuff in Mac OS X, but this chapter will help you exorcise those demons fast!

STOPPING THE SOFTWARE AUTO-UPDATING MENACE

The idea is great—whenever a new piece of software is released to update your existing software, a window pops up to tell you that it's been released, and it even offers to go download the software for you. The problem? It always, always opens at the wrong time: when you're on deadline, when you're five minutes from leaving the office—really, any time you don't want it to pop up—it pops up. Personally, I'd rather decide to update at my leisure (once a week or so) rather than when my System feels it needs a fix. To turn off this Auto-Updating menace, go under the Apple menu to System Preferences. Click on the Software Update icon, and where it says "Update Software," make sure to turn off "Automatically check for updates when you have a network connection." Or you can choose to be interrupted at the wrong time only once a month (from the pop-up menu). Either way "Another one bites the dust!"

PUTTING SNAPZ PRO CAPTURES WHERE YOU WANT THEM

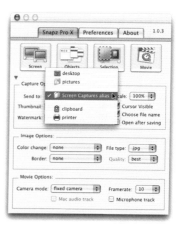

Snapz Pro is a wonderful screen capture utility that comes bundled with Mac OS X (at least, with versions 10.2 and higher). I love Snapz Pro, and the version for Mac OS X is their best version yet. With the exception of one incredibly annoying thing—you can only save your captures in one of two places: on your desktop or in your Pictures folder. (In previous versions, you could save your captures anywhere you wanted.) Well, here's the fix: Click on the folder on your drive where you'd like your screen captures to appear (I named mine, surprisingly enough, "Screen Captures"). Then, press Command-L to make an alias of this folder. Now drag this alias into your Pictures folder. That's it! This Alias folder will now appear in Snapz Pro's "Send to" pop-up menu. Now, when you save your captures in this Alias folder, they will actually appear in the original Screen Captures folder you designated. It sounds more complicated than it is—try it once, and you'll use it all the time.

IT WON'T LET ME ERASE MY DISK!

In all previous versions of the Mac OS, when you wanted to erase a disk, you just went under the Special menu and chose Erase Disk. But in Mac OS X, there is no Special menu (Apple might counter that all the menus are special—they're not). Now to erase a disk, you have to launch Disk Utility (inside your Utilities folder on your hard drive). When you launch Disk Utility, just click on the tab for "Erase" and you're there!

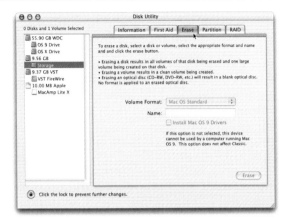

  STOP MAGNIFYING

This may be a very embarrassing subject for some of you, so I'll try to handle it with the utmost sensitivity. If you have very small Dock icons (and you know who you are) the Magnification feature is almost a necessity. However, if you leave your Dock icons at their default size (which many people do) magnification can be wildly annoying and since the icons are so large to begin with, magnification is totally unnecessary. When my wife first saw large Dock icons being magnified even more, the first thing she said was, "Is there a way to turn that awful thing off?" There is: Go under the Apple menu, under Dock, and choose "Turn Magnification Off."

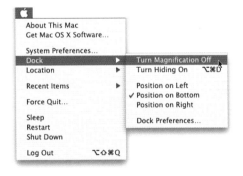

DO YOU REALLY WANT TO EMPTY THE TRASH?

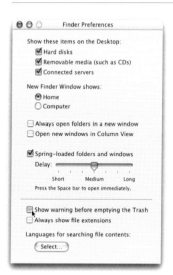

There's nothing like executing a simple command, and having the OS ask "Are you sure you want to do this?" By default, every time you go to Empty the Trash, it asks this annoying question (and it has for years upon years). Disabling the "Empty Trash Warning" is a little different in Mac OS X than it was in previous versions. Now you go under the Finder menu, under Preferences, and uncheck the checkbox for: "Show warning before emptying Trash."

   ## DELETING LOCKED FILES

Mac OS X is much tougher about your trying to delete a locked file. In fact, you can't pull that "drop it in the trash, hold the Option key, and choose 'Empty Trash'" routine, because Mac OS X won't even let you put it in the Trash in the first place. You have to unlock it manually by clicking on the file and pressing Command-L to bring up the Info window. Then uncheck the checkbox for Locked. Now it's yours for the trashing.

STOP ASKING ME WHAT TO DO!

There's a feature in Mac OS X that's both a blessing and a curse (it's a blessing if it does what you want, but otherwise...). For example, when you insert a blank CD it brings up a dialog box asking what you want to do with it. Chances are, you do the same thing over and over (prepare it for burning, launch Toast, launch iTunes, etc.), but it keeps asking you, again and again, every time you insert a CD. It's just this side of maddening. You can change Mac OS X's list of "when you insert this, I'm opening that..." by going under the Apple menu, under System Preferences, and choosing CDs & DVDs. There you'll find a plain-English list of pop-up menus that lets you stop opening any applications that you don't want, and you can choose which apps, if any, you do want opened. Most importantly, Mac OS X will stop asking you what to do.

   DEALING WITH THE COMMAND-N NO-FOLDER BLUES

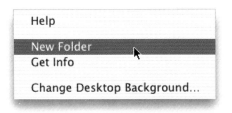

Okay, we have to deal with the fact that Command-N no longer creates a new folder. It's always been that way, we liked it that way, but I guess Apple just had to "mess with our heads" this time around. The fastest way around this frightening catastrophe is to Control-click in an open area of your window (or desktop) and choose New Folder from the short pop-up menu that appears. I know, I know, it's no Command-N, but that's about the quickest way. I know, you could put a New Folder icon in the Toolbar, but then it's not really a keyboard shortcut anymore, is it?

   HIDING THE ANNOYING MICROPHONE DISC THINGY

I cover this tip elsewhere in the book, but since this is so annoying, I knew you'd be looking for it in this chapter too. When you open an application that supports Mac OS X's built-in Speech control (like Chess for instance), it brings up what I call "the incredibly annoying round microphone thingy." It floats around, taking up space, and if you're not using Speech control (which most of us aren't), it's just plain annoying. If you are actually using Speech control, it's still annoying (necessary perhaps, but still annoying). To get it out of sight, double-click on the top half of it, and it will tuck itself into the Dock while you work.

   MAKING THE ANNOYING ALERT SOUND LESS ANNOYING

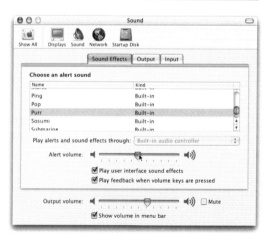

Do you find the default alert sound annoying? Oh yeah, after a few days its very sound sends blood trickling down my ear (okay, that's a bit of an exaggeration, but only a bit). You can change it to a different sound, but that would stop just short of what it really needs—to be much quieter (unless, of course, you're using your Mac on a noisy factory floor). To change sounds and lower the Alert volume, go under the System Preferences and click on the Sound icon. When it appears, click on the Sound Effects tab, and then you can hear each alert tone by clicking on it. Find the one that makes you shudder the least and then, most importantly, use the Alert volume slider to set it at a volume that doesn't take your head off every time you make a little mistake. Ahhhh. That's better, isn't it?

STOPPING THE OVERLY POLITE DOCK ICONS

If you're trying to drag-and-drop a document into a folder icon on the Dock, but instead of letting you drop it, all the icons scoot out of the way (they think you're trying 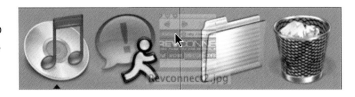 to add the icon to the Dock, rather than dropping it on the folder icon you want to add the file to)—there's a way to make them stay put: Just hold the Command key before you drag the file and the Dock icons will stay right where they are.

STOP ASKING ME FOR MY PASSWORD

Are you like me? No. Then how about this: Are you like me in the sense that you're the only person that works on your Mac? Maybe it's your Mac at home, and not a single soul but you uses your machine (meaning, of course, your spouse, your kids, and the cat all have their own Macs). Then you don't need an administrator to tell you what you can and can't add to your own single, solitary machine, right? It's just you. And  you're a good person. Then when you install Mac OS X, and it asks you for an administrator password, don't put one in. Leave it blank, and that way, you'll never have to remember your password. Oh sure, it'll try to tell you that you may have a security problem (the cat might try to sneak a virus on your machine), but if you're the only one who will ever install a program on that machine, wouldn't you love to just click the OK button when the annoying password dialog pops up the next time you want to install a program?

STOP THE POPPIN' DOCK (AT LEAST FOR NOW)

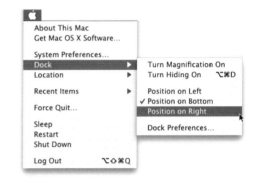

The Dock's hiding feature can be really helpful, until you launch an application that takes over the full screen (such as iMovie or Final Cut Pro). The problem occurs when you go to use part of the application that's near the bottom of the screen (like the Timeline) and the Dock keeps popping up in your way. This may sound too simple, but when you're using iMovie, Final Cut Pro, or any other app that has you working near the bottom of your screen, just go under the Apple menu, under Dock, and choose Position on Right. This temporarily moves the Dock to the right side of your monitor, eliminating the problem. When you quit the application, simply switch your Dock back to the bottom.

SAVE TIME WHEN LAUNCHING PROGRAMS—NEVER QUIT!

Isn't it annoying how long it takes applications to launch? Oh sure, they launch faster in Mac OS X, but it's still annoying to wait for them to open, isn't it? The fix: don't quit your applications. Because Mac OS X manages its memory so well, you can leave the applications you use most open all the time—there's no major advantage to quitting after you're done working in them (like there was back in Mac OS 9). They just don't take up the resources, or put much of a strain on your computer, so quitting them doesn't really help. (Note: This is for Mac OS X apps only—not Classic Apps.) Many experts also recommend that you don't shut down your Mac; rather just put it to sleep, because the UNIX core of Mac OS X was designed to run all day and all night, and shutting it down just isn't necessary (unless, of course, you live where I do in Florida, where the next thunderstorm is usually just a few hours away, especially in summer, in which case not only do I shut down, I run around my house unplugging everything in sight).

   PUTTING THE GENIE BACK IN HIS BOTTLE

Certainly the Genie Effect (which is that genie-like special effect which occurs by default when you minimize a window to the Dock) would be a nominee for the "Mac OS X Annoying Hall of Fame." Luckily, putting this Genie back in his bottle is easy—just go under the Apple menu, under System Preferences, and when the prefs dialog appears, click on Dock. In the Dock Preferences pane, in the pop-up

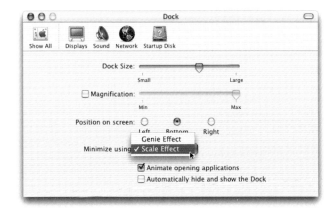

menu for Minimize using, choose Scale Effect rather than Genie, and that should put a cork in it (so to speak).

   BECOMING A CIVILIAN AGAIN

I never had the honor of serving in the military, so I never got used to the 24-hour military clock. Unfortunately, that's what showed up in my Menu Bar, for some strange reason, for two solid weeks after I first installed Mac OS X (before Jaguar, back at version 10.1). Back then I searched, and searched, but I could not find out where to change the 24-hour clock back to the 12-hour clock. I finally had to look it up in a book, and I was stunned to find that the control for this was not in the System Preference for Date & Time— that just makes way too much sense; instead, it was in the International System Preferences

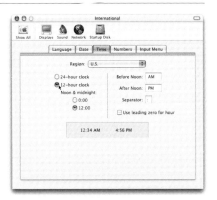

(perhaps because many foreign countries use the 24-hour clock. How "un-American"). At that point, I looked at my Mac and said out loud, "Okay, you beat me." Luckily, in Jaguar, it's somewhat easier, because at least now it's also found in the regular Date & Time System Preference, but it's still a bit buried. Rather than putting it in the Date & Time tab, instead you have to look under the Menu Bar Clock tab, where you'll find a checkbox where you can turn off "Use a 24-hour clock."

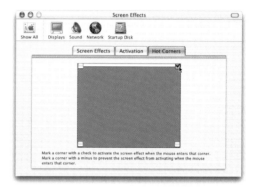

DISABLING SCREEN SAVER HOT CORNERS

Does your Screen Saver keep turning on when you rest your cursor in one of the corners of your screen? Well, this used to drive me crazy (I say used to, because I used this tip to fix it). What's happening is that one of your corners has been designated as a "Hot Corner" (at least as far as Mac OS X's screen saver is concerned), and whenever your cursor winds up there for more than a second or two it starts Mac OS X's built-in screen saver. To make this "Hot Corner" stuff go away, go to the System Preferences, and click on the Screen Effects icon. When its pane appears, click on the Hot Corners tab. When it appears, you'll see little checkboxes in each dialog that represents your screen. If one or more of these checkboxes has a checkmark in it, those are the current Hot Corners. Just click twice directly on this "x" to clear any checked checkboxes, until all four checkboxes are clear, making your "Hot Corners" go cold, and the full screen is now yours to enjoy uninterrupted.

 ## SLEEP LESS—WORK MORE

Have you plugged your PowerBook or iBook into an A/C outlet, but it's still going to sleep on you every five or ten minutes? Honestly, that drives me nuts, and if you're like me, once you plug in, you'll want to go to the System Preferences and click on the Energy Saver icon. When its pane appears, click on the Sleep tab (if you don't see the tab, click on the Show Details button on the bottom right), and then drag the slider over to a reasonable amount of time (like 30 minutes or more). That way, if you do call it a night and forget to put your PowerBook to sleep, eventually Energy Saver will kick in.

STOP THE BOUNCING. I BEG YOU!

When you launch an
application, its icon begins
to bounce incessantly in
the Dock, in a distracting
vertical Tigger-like motion,
until the app is just about
open. I love this feature;
but then, I enjoy having my
cavities drilled. If you
enjoy this animation as
much as I do, you can turn
it off by going to the Apple
menu, under Dock, and
choosing Dock Preferences.
When the Dock Preferences

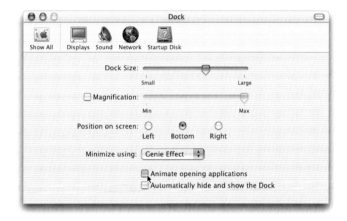

pane appears, turn off the checkbox (it's on by default) for "Animate opening applications." Turning this off now can save you thousands in therapy costs down the road.

    SHUTTING DOWN WITHOUT THE WARNING

When you choose Shut
Down from the Apple
menu, a dialog box
appears asking if you
really want to shut
down. Yes, it's annoying.
To make the bad dialog
box go away, just hold
the Option key before
you choose Shut Down,

and it will just Shut Down (without insulting your intelligence by asking you if what you
chose is really what you want to do).

     STOPPING QUICKTIME FROM UPDATING

If there's one piece of software that seems to be getting a tiny tweak about once a week, it's QuickTime. Of course, that's not the case at all, it just seems that way, because the little window that pops up to tell you there's been an update to QuickTime seems to be popping up all the time. (Again, it's not—it just seems that way.) To stop the update alert madness, go under the Apple menu, under System Preferences, and click on the QuickTime icon. In the QuickTime pane, click on the Update tab and turn off the checkbox called

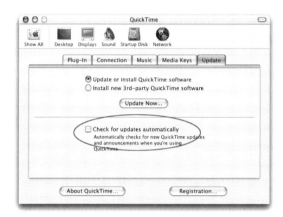

"Check for updates automatically." Now you're on your honor to go and check for them yourself, at least six to ten times a day (kidding).

Apple really pulled off an amazing feat by nesting a version of Mac OS 9 right within Mac OS X so you can still run applications that haven't

Hooked on Classics
tips for using the classic environment

yet been updated to run in Mac OS X. When you think about it, it's really brilliant. Once you use it, you'll find that it runs those applications surprisingly well. Once you begin to use it often, it won't be long before you hate the Classic Environment with every fiber of your being. Just seeing the Classic Environment start-up bar can set into motion a vexing combination of facial tics, with an uncontrollable urge to shout obscenities that make no sense whatsoever (stuff like "Eat my mandible, you shoe-wearing turquoise trailer-hitch"). In short, you quickly start to dedicate every waking hour, and all your available resources to never, ever, having to use the Classic Environment. But until you reach that ultimate nirvana, where all of your applications run in an operating system actually released in the 21st century, here are some tips to keep your temporary bouts of Tourette's Syndrome in check while working in Classic.

OPENING MAC OS X APPS IN CLASSIC MODE

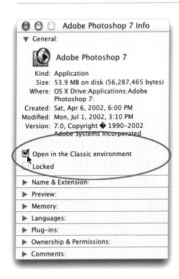

A number of applications (Apple calls them "Carbon" apps) will run in either Mac OS X or Classic mode (such as Adobe Photoshop 7.0), but by default, they're going to launch in Mac OS X (and why not? OS X is a much better operating system). However, there may be instances where you want the application to launch in Classic mode (for example, if you can't get a printer or scanner to work in Mac OS X, you might need to have the application open in Classic so you can access printing/scanning). To launch a Mac OS X app in Classic mode, just click on the application's icon and press Command-I. When the Info window appears, you'll see a checkbox for "Open in the Classic Environment." Click on the checkbox, close the window, launch the application, and it will open in Classic. Don't forget that you've done this little wizardry, or it will always open in Classic, so go back and "uncheck" that box when you're ready to relaunch it in Mac OS X.

   START CLASSIC MODE EVERY TIME AUTOMATICALLY

If you use Classic mode apps every day (and I feel bad for you if you have to), then you might want Mac OS X to launch Classic mode automatically for you whenever you start up your Mac. You can do that by going under the Apple menu, under System Preferences, and clicking on the Classic icon. When its pane appears, click on the Start/ Stop tab, then click the checkbox for "Start Classic when you log in," which is a very un-Apple-like way of saying, "when I start my computer, go ahead and start Classic too." I've always felt that someone who used to work at Microsoft came up with that checkbox description, but I can't prove it.

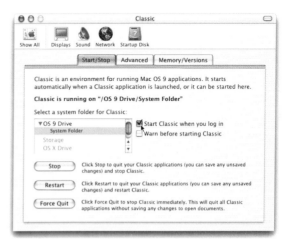

ONE-CLICK DESKTOP REBUILDING

If you've been using the Mac for years, no doubt you're familiar with the concept of "rebuilding the desktop" in Mac OS 9. It's one of those things you do once a month, whether you need it or not, to keep everything running smoothly, to keep your icons looking right, plus a host of other good things. You used to rebuild the desktop by holding Option-Command while booting your computer, but now you don't have to (especially since holding Option-Command while booting in Mac OS X won't rebuild your Classic desktop). Now, it's easier than ever. Just go under the

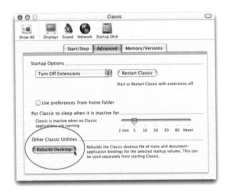

Apple menu, choose System Preferences, and click on the Classic icon. When its pane appears, click on the Advanced tab, and the advanced features pane will appear with a Rebuild Desktop button (at the bottom of the pane). Just click it, and it does its thing. You don't even have to restart Classic—just click the button.

   ## YOU DON'T HAVE TO LAUNCH CLASSIC TO REBUILD ITS DESKTOP

This may sound pretty weird at first, especially if you're a longtime Mac user; but you don't actually have to be in the Classic Environment to rebuild its desktop. That's right, just go under the Mac OS X Apple menu, under System Preferences, and click on the Classic icon. In the pane that appears, click the Advanced tab, and then click the Rebuild Desktop button. The Mac does its thing (the rebuilding, that is) while you're still in Mac OS X, without running the Classic Environment. Freaky.

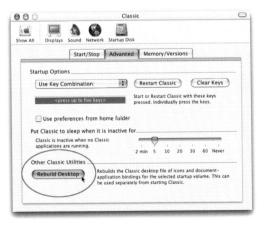

GETTING RID OF JAGGY DOCK ICONS

Mac OS X doesn't put an icon in the Dock to
let you know when you're running an application in Classic mode, but it does give you a hint;
it makes the icon for your Classic application
look really ratty and jaggy. Well, you might not
notice how ratty these icons look if you have

your Dock icons set to a fairly small size. But if they're large, or you give them a glance
when you roll your cursor over them and they're magnified, you'll notice that those
Classic icons look totally ratty at those larger sizes (while your cool OS X icons look great
at any size). The way around this? Even though those old apps run in Classic mode, you
can still copy and paste OS X-style icons over their original icons (so at least you won't
have to live with the jaggies). You can download some of these icons from various Web
sites such as www.iconfactory.com or www.xicon.macnn.com, where they've got loads of
Mac OS X-savvy icons. To copy an icon, click on it in the Finder and press Command-I.
When the Info window pops up, press Command-C to copy the icon. Then, go to the
Applications (Mac OS 9) folder, click on the app whose jaggy icon drives you nuts, click on
the still-open Info window to make it active, and press Command-V to paste your new
icon right over the old one. Now, the next time you run this Classic app, take a look in
your Dock and a wonderfully clean icon will appear there. Ahhhh, that's better.

   NOT ALL CLASSIC CONTROL PANELS WORK

If you're a longtime Mac user, you're
used to working with Mac OS 9.x's
Control Panels, and that's why I want
to warn you not to get upset when you
choose them in Classic mode and many
of their functions appear grayed out.
That's because those functions are now
handled by Mac OS X, and shouldn't be
addressed by both OSs (is that a word?
OSs? Or is it OSes, or OS's? Better yet,

does anyone really care?). For example, you don't want to set the time in Classic and
then have a different time, off by a few seconds perhaps, in Mac OS X mode.
So, for your own sanity, some of these Control Panel items are grayed out.

HOW TO TELL IF IT'S A CLASSIC APP OR NOT

Sure, once the application is fully launched and its icon appears in the Dock, you can usually tell if it's a Classic app and not a Mac OS X app by its jaggy icon. But if you'd rather know before you go through the Classic launch cycle, just click on the app's icon, and press Command-I. When the Info window appears, look at the "Kind" field. If it's a Classic app, it'll say so right here.

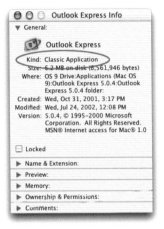

  GIVE CLASSIC APPS MAC OS X MEMORY POWER!

If you've used Mac OS 9 for a while, you already know how to assign memory to individual applications, and you do it the same way today in Classic. You just click on the Classic app's icon, press Command-I, and up pops the Info window. Click the right-facing gray triangle at the left of the word "Memory" to expand that pane. Enter the amount of memory you'd like the app to have in the Preferred Size field. (For the best performance, make sure it's more than the amount shown as its Suggested Size. In fact, to really take advantage of Mac OS X's new memory management, you need to increase this amount by quite a bit, so go memory-hog wild.)

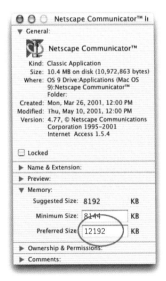

   WANT MORE THAN ONE CLASSIC SYSTEM FOLDER? GO FOR IT!

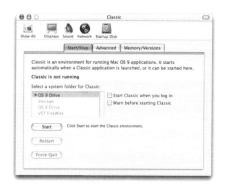

Back before Mac OS X, having more than one System Folder was akin to driving on the freeway totally blindfolded—big problems are right around the corner. It was just something you didn't do, and if a Mac consultant found more than one system on your machine, they would berate you till you were on the ground in the fetal position. But now, everything's different. If you want one trimmed-down system for running a couple of Classic apps, but then want the option of booting a separate OS 9.2 system packed with every Control Panel and Extension known to man, it's totally cool. There's just one thing you really have to do to keep things running smoothly: Make sure that these other systems either reside on a totally separate hard drive, or partition your drive so the other system appears on a different partition. Once that's done, go under the Apple menu, under System Preferences, and click on the Classic icon. In this pane, you'll see a list of drives you can boot from (under the heading, "Select a system folder for Classic"). Choose the drive that has the system you want to use, then click the Start button.

   IF OS X WANTS TO ADD STUFF TO CLASSIC, LET IT

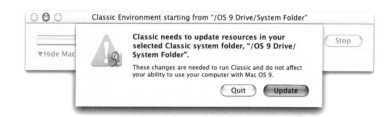

The first time you launch Classic mode, a warning dialog may appear telling you "Some Classic-specific resources need to be added or updated in your system folder." It asks, "Do you want to add or update them?" and it gives you two choices: Quit or Update. This freaks out a lot of people, because it sounds as if they themselves will be responsible for determining which these are, and installing them. But if you click Update, Mac OS will do all the dirty work for you, and your only involvement in this process is clicking that Update button to start the process (which only takes a few seconds). So, in short, it's OK to press the Update button.

STOPPING A CLASSIC LAUNCH

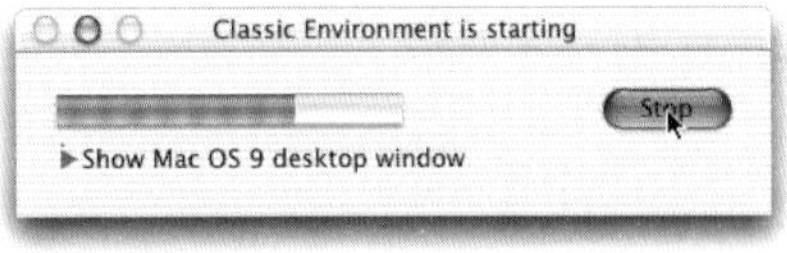

There's nothing more aggravating than accidentally launching the Classic Environment and having to sit there waiting for the whole thing to load, just so you can quit. If that happens, you can press the "Stop" button, but you'll get a scary-looking warning dialog box trying to convince you not to stop now, but to wait until the whole thing launches, then switch to Mac OS X, go under the Apple menu to access the System Preferences and quit it there. Yeah, I've got time to do that. After you've done this once or twice (sat through the whole aggravating process, etc.), you'll finally start hitting the Stop button. It will stop immediately, and although you're flying in the face of a very scary warning dialog, you'll be glad to know many people have been doing this for quite a while, and they have still gone on to lead successful and productive lives. In short: we hit that Stop button any time we accidentally launch Classic.

SLEEPY JUICE

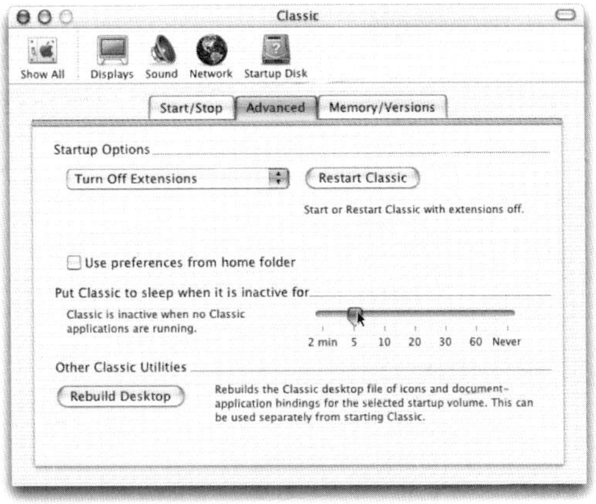

Once you've launched Classic, there's no real reason to quit it, except maybe to free up some memory; but if you have to restart Classic, you have to wait for the whole darn thing to load again. Instead of doing that, you can put Classic to sleep. Putting Classic to sleep is like putting a PowerBook to sleep—it's still launched, but it's kind of in the background, and barely taking up any valuable system resources. To put Classic to sleep, go under the Apple menu, under System Preferences, or click System Preferences in the dock, then click on the Classic icon. When the Classic pane appears, click on the Advanced pane, and you'll see a slider where you can reduce the time before it sleeps to two minutes (I know, where's the "sleep now" button?). Close any open Classic apps, and in a couple of minutes, Classic finally nods off. To wake it up, just scream at your computer. If that doesn't work, just open a Classic application. It takes a few seconds to wake up (just like waking up a PowerBook in OS 9.2), but it beats the heck out of launching Classic all over again.

   SKIPPING MAC OS X ALTOGETHER: STARTING IN MAC OS 9.X

If you need to start up in Mac OS 9.2 (rather than starting in Mac OS X as usual), go under the Apple menu or to the Dock, choose System Preferences, and choose Startup Disk. You'll have a choice of starting up with either OS 9 or Mac OS X. Click on OS 9, then click on the Restart button, and it's like pushing a button to a time warp. At

least that's the way you'll feel after running Mac OS X with its beautiful Aqua look and feel. When you launch Mac OS 9.2, it feels so, well...old-fashioned.

   THE COPY AND PASTE PAUSE THAT REFRESHES

You can copy data from an application in the Classic Environment and paste it into an application in Mac OS X, but if you do, expect a small delay (just a second or two) before the pasted data appears. That's because it takes OS X a few moments to "chunk" on the data before it's ready to paste, so don't freak out if it doesn't paste as quickly as you're used to in Mac OS X. In fact, if you try pasting and it doesn't work, you might have to paste it a second time.

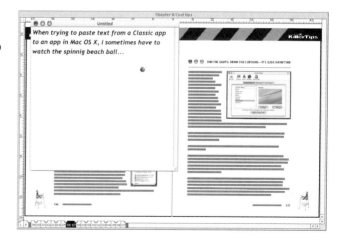

SAVING BEFORE YOU QUIT CLASSIC

If you've got half a dozen Classic applications open with one or two documents in each, what happens if you quit Classic mode? All is well, as long as you quit in a civilized way by switching to the Mac OS X Finder (use the Finder icon in the Dock), going under the Apple menu, and choosing System Preferences. Click on the Classic icon, and in the pane that appears, just press the Stop button. Classic mode will quit, but it will give you a chance to save any open, unsaved documents running in Classic. However, if you choose Quit and Classic doesn't quit, you can choose Force Quit from the Apple menu (or

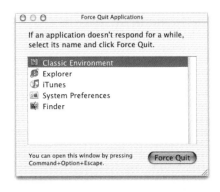

pressing Option-Command-Esc), but doing that will quit all applications and close all open documents without saving them first, so think twice about force quitting Classic.

   ## GETTING CLASSIC TO START UP FASTER

Do you want the Classic environment to start up faster? (I know, that may be the stupidest question of the year. Really, who *doesn't* want Classic mode to start faster?) Then all you have to do is disable any extraneous Extensions and Control Panels you may have had running when you upgraded to Mac OS X. (If you brought a brand-new machine with Mac OS X pre-loaded, you may not run into this problem as much.) To disable any extra Extensions and Control Panels,

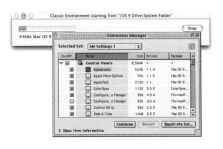

choose System Preferences under the Apple Menu and click on the Classic icon. In the Classic pane, click on the Advanced tab. In the pop-up menu in the Startup Options section at the top, choose "Open Extensions Manager" and then click on the "Restart Classic" button right next to the pop-up. As Classic is starting up the Extensions Manager will appear (just like the old days, eh?) and you can then choose which of these goodies you can live without. Not sure which ones you can pitch? Try using the Base set (just the Extensions that are necessary to start the system) from the pop-up menu.

 CAN'T REMEMBER THE CLASSIC KEYBOARD SHORTCUT?

Can't remember all the little keyboard shortcuts to "tweak" Classic mode? Neither can I. That's probably why Apple replaced most of those Classic keyboard shortcuts (at least the ones you're used to when you launched Mac OS 9 anyway) with one-click buttons and pop-up menus. You'll find these under the Apple menu, under System Preferences, under Classic. When the Classic pane appears, click on the Advanced tab, and you'll see options for little shortcuts (such as bringing up the Extensions Manager during startup, rebuilding your desktop, etc.).

 RESTART MANUALLY TO PURGE MEMORY

If the Classic Environment quits on you (hey, it happens), just relaunch it by going under the OS X Finder, under System Preferences, clicking on the Classic icon, and in the pane that appears, click on the Start button. Doing it this way will purge the memory automatically and help to keep the problem from recurring.

RESTARTING CLASSIC WITH KEYBOARD SHORTCUTS

Remember all the keyboard shortcuts you could use when you were starting up your Mac in OS 9 for such things as starting with the Extensions off or rebuilding your desktop? Well, these shortcuts are still there for the Classic Environment but it's not as simple as just holding the keys anymore. Here's how: Go under the Apple menu, under System Preferences, and click on the Classic icon. When the pane appears, click on the Advanced tab, and in the pop-up menu under Startup Options, choose "Use Key Combination." Then simply type in the keyboard shortcut

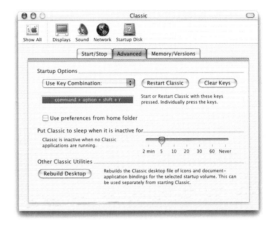

you want to use (e.g., the Shift key to start with Extensions off). Now, click on the "Restart Classic" button right next to the pop-up. Classic will restart as if you were physically holding these keys. Note: These shortcuts will only work when you start Classic the slow way—from the Classic pane itself.

ONE-CLICK CLASSIC MODE

Apple decided not to put the Classic mode icon in the Dock while you're running Classic mode apps. Maybe it's because they didn't want early Mac OS X adopters to realize how many times they'd have to be running apps in Classic mode (hey, it's just a guess), but nonetheless, it's not there. However, some people (mostly freaks) like to have the Classic icon appear in the Dock (okay, it's not just freaks. But it's mostly freaks). If you're one of "those" people (you know who you are), you can add the Classic icon to your Dock by double-clicking on your hard drive icon, then look inside the folder named "System" (the one with the "X" on it, not the one named "System Folder" with a 9 on it), then look inside the "Library" folder, and inside that you'll find a folder named "CoreServices." In this folder is a file named "Classic Startup." Drag this icon onto the Dock and then if you feel like taking a "time tunnel" back to the past, you're only one click away.

  THE CARBON ADVANTAGE

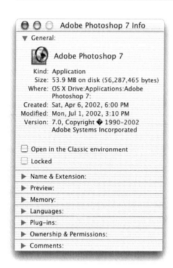

There are basically two different kinds of applications in regard to Mac OS X: Carbonized applications (which are apps that were originally designed for Mac OS 9, and the developer has just created an update that runs in Mac OS X) or Cocoa apps (which have a light chocolaty taste. Okay, they're actually applications that have been written for Mac OS X from the ground up, *and* they have a light chocolaty taste). It's helpful to know this because Carbonized applications have the distinct advantage of being able to be run in *either* Mac OS X or the Classic Environment. See the tip earlier in this chapter on how to make a Carbonized app run in Classic when launched.

   WHERE IS THE CLASSIC FINDER/DESKTOP?

Because of the way Mac OS X works, you can't see the Classic Finder/ desktop. The only way to see it again is to have your Mac ignore Mac OS X's Finder altogether by restarting your Mac in Mac OS 9.2. You do this in the System Prefer- ences under Startup Disk.

CAN'T REMEMBER WHETHER CLASSIC IS RUNNING?

If you can't remember whether Classic is running or not, just go under the Apple menu (or to the Dock), under System Preferences, and click on the Classic icon. In the pane that appears, if the Classic Environment is running, you'll see the message "Classic is running" on the drive that it's running on.

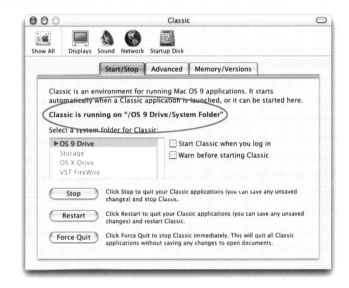

SWITCHING APPS IN CLASSIC

If you want to switch between applications while running the Classic environment, you do it the same way you would back before Mac OS X—click on the application's name in the upper right-hand corner of your screen, and choose the currently running application you want to switch to from the pop-up menu. The cool thing is, any Mac OS X applications will be listed there too, so you can choose to switch to either Classic or Mac OS X applications from this pop-up menu.

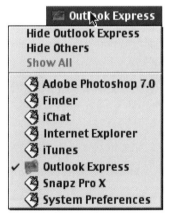

   RUNNING APPS THAT WON'T RUN IN CLASSIC

If you haven't already, you will almost certainly run across an application that simply won't run in Classic mode or Mac OS X. You know it won't because you'll get a little warning dialog telling you "the application is not supported." When that happens, what you'll have to do is change your Startup System to Mac OS 9.2

and restart. This is just one of those cases where Mac OS X's Classic emulator just isn't enough. Luckily, these instances are few and far between, but now at least when you run across one, you'll know what to do, eh?

   FORCE QUITTING CLASSIC MODE

If for some reason Classic just won't quit when you choose Stop from the Classic preferences (found in the System Preferences by clicking on the Classic icon), then you can press Option-Command-Esc. This brings up the Force Quit Applications pane, and you'll see an item in the list named "Classic Environment." Click on that, then click the Force Quit button, which will force Classic to quit.

JUMPING TO CLASSIC MODE, WHEN YOU CHARGE BY THE HOUR

You probably already know that the fastest way to get into Classic mode is to double-click on a document created in a Classic application. Mac OS X will automatically launch Classic mode for you, launch the application, and open your document (hey, if you didn't know that, there's another tip!). But if you don't want to do it the fast way, there is another slower, more "billable-hours" way: go under the Apple menu, under System Preference, and click on the Classic icon. Its pane will appear, where you can click on the button marked "Start."

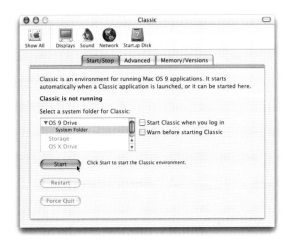

CLASSIC SPEED TIP: TURN OFF THE FUNKY SOUNDS

Mac OS 9.x offered you the ability to add a "soundtrack" to your Mac life. If you clicked on something, it made a sound. Open a window—another sound. Scrolled through a window— more sounds. They were cute at first, but most users turned them off after just a few days. Those who chose to leave them on had to be institutionalized after hearing these sounds for just a few weeks. Well, now there's a new reason to turn them off—it slows things down. To turn off the annoying

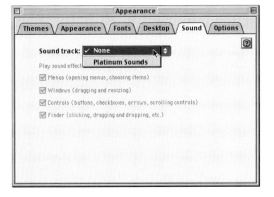

soundtrack, while in Classic go under the Apple menu, under Control Panels, and choose Appearance. Click on the Sound tab, and from the Sound track pop-up menu choose None.

If I could show you some Mac OS X speed tips that would make you faster and more productive at Mac OS X than you ever dreamed possible,

Fly Like an Eagle
mac os x speed tips

how much would you be willing to pay? 50 bucks? 75 bucks? 100 bucks? Easily. So basically, by paying a list price of only $29.99 for this book, I figure you're ahead by at least $10.05 (if you said 50 bucks) and possibly as much as $60.05 (if you said 100 bucks). Well, if you think about it, although many of the tips in this book will make you faster, only this particular chapter is on speed tips, so in reality, you were willing to pay between $50 and $100 for just the tips in the this chapter, so technically, you should've paid extra for the other chapters. Now granted, they won't all make you faster, so I'm willing to give you a discount—$10 a chapter—so add $120 (there are 12 other chapters) onto the $60.05 you already owe, making your total value around $180.05. Now, if you ordered this book from Amazon.com, and got 30% off the list price, you're just flat taking advantage of the situation, and to make up for it, I expect you to feel a level of guilt that is commensurate with the value actually received.

   IS THAT TASK DONE YET? THE DOCK KNOWS...

Let's say you're working in a power-crunching app like Photoshop, and you go to apply a filter to a high-res image, and it's going to take a minute or two to process your command. You're going to get a progress bar so you can see how long the process is going to take, right? Well, thanks to Mac OS X's way-cool Dock, you can switch out of Photoshop and work on something else, and the Dock will let you know when the filter is applied. How? Well, when a progress bar appears in Photoshop, the Dock automatically adds a tiny little progress bar to the bottom of the Photoshop icon in the Dock so you can keep an eye on the progress, even when you're doing something else (like checking your mail, shopping online, or writing a letter).

   CHANGING WHICH APP OPENS WHICH DOC

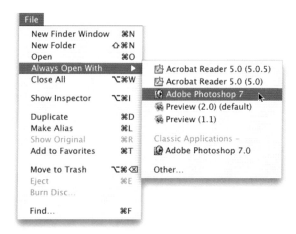

If you have a file, let's say it's a graphics file in PICT format, by default it will open in Preview, right? And you probably know that you can go into the file's Info window and reassign that file to open in a different application; but there's an easier way. Just click on the PICT file, go under the File menu and choose "Open With" and choose the app you want to open that particular file (I would choose Photoshop, but hey, that's just me). If you decide you always want PICT Files to open in a different app (such as Photoshop) hold the Option key first, and when you go under the File menu you'll see that the menu item name "Open With" has changed to "Always Open With."

SAVING TIME IN SAVE AS

Here's a fairly wild Mac OS X tip for saving a
file (this is a great one to show at parties.
Well, at least parties where there are lots of
Mac-heads). If you're going to save a document
and you can see the folder on your drive where
you want to save it (it's in a Finder window
or on your desktop), in the Save As Sheet,
expand the Column View by clicking on the
blue button with the down-facing triangle.
Then you can actually drag-and-drop the folder
that you want to save your document in from
the desktop or Finder window to one of the
columns in your Save As Sheet. This is one of
those things you have to try once yourself, but
once you do, you'll use it again and again to
save time when saving documents.

   INSTANT COLUMN RESIZING

If you're in Column View, you can get tired
of resizing columns to accommodate long
filenames. But Mac OS X can do this for you.
Just double-click on any resizing tab
(they're the two little vertical lines at the
bottom of each column), and that will
automatically expand all the columns to
accommodate the longest filename that
appears in any column. Pretty sweet!

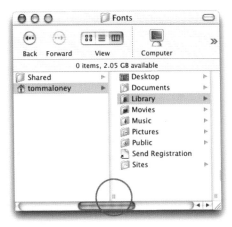

LAUNCH IT, THEN CLOSE ITS WINDOW

While in Icon or List View, if you launch an app or open a document that launches an app from a Finder window (rather than from the Dock), hold the Option key as you launch it, and the window you launched from will automatically close. It kind of tidies up for you as you go.

QUICK QUITTING SPEED TIP

You can quickly quit any program without actually going to that program. Hold the Command key and press the Tab key until the program's icon appears highlighted in the Dock, and then press the letter "q" and it will quit. (Okay, this is

kind of cheating: since you already have Command held down, you don't have to press it again, so you're really pressing Command-Q).

   NEED TO CHECK SOMETHING OUT? HIDE YOUR APP FAST

If you're working in an application and want to hide it from view (you're not quitting here—just hiding it from view), press Command-H. This is handy if you need to see something in a Finder window or check something out from another open app. To make your application reappear, just click on its

icon in the Dock, or press Command-Tab until its icon appears highlighted in the Dock, then release Command-Tab and the app will be visible once again.

   DOCUMENT ALIASES—THE FAST WAY

Want to quickly create an alias for the document or folder you're working on? Just press Option-Command and then click-and-hold on the tiny icon that appears to the left of the document's name in the document's title bar and drag that little icon to your desktop. (By the way, that "tiny little icon" is technically called "the proxy icon," but that's just so...technical-sounding.)

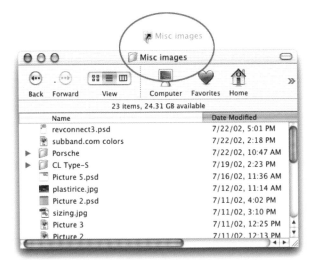

MOVING A FILE OUT OF A FOLDER IN LIST VIEW

Let's say you're in List View, and the file you want is inside a folder you see in the list (hey, this is going pretty good so far). You expand the folder, start scrolling, and way down near the bottom of the folder's list is the file you want. To get that file out of the folder it's in and place it in the original window (before you expanded the folder), you'll have to do a lot of scrolling. In fact, you'll have to scroll back up until you get to an area before where the folder appears, so you can drop the icon outside the folder. But there's a quicker way that requires no scrolling: just drag the icon of the document you want to remove from the folder straight up to the headers along the top of the columns. A little line of whatever color you've chosen for your highlight will appear along the bottom of the column headers to let you know "you're there"). Release the mouse button, and your file will now appear as a separate item, outside the folder, with the other items in the list.

GET THAT FIRST ICON FAST

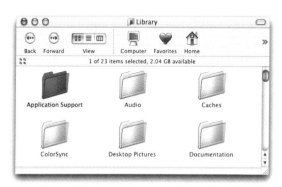

If you've opened a Finder document window in Icon View and want to select the first document (alphabetically), just press Tab and it will instantly become highlighted. If you want the last file (alphabetically) in the window, press Shift-Tab.

FASTER RENAMING IN LIST VIEW

Remember that tip, many chapters ago, for quickly renaming an icon (you know—click on the icon and then press the Return key to highlight the naming field)? Well, if you're in List View, you don't have to go through all that—just click directly on the file's name (rather than its tiny icon), and in just a moment the name field will highlight for you—almost begging for a new name to be typed in. This works in Column View too—but you have to click on the file's name once to highlight it, then click once more and the name field becomes active.

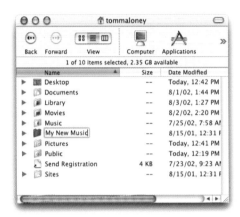

   WAIT! I DIDN'T MEAN TO DRAG THAT!

I've done this a million times (okay, not a million, but at least 640,000 times)—I've been in a Finder window, and I started dragging an icon to somewhere else in the window and then I realize that I either: (a) grabbed the wrong icon, (b) changed my mind, or (c) changed my mind when I realized I grabbed the wrong icon. If you were to let go of the mouse button—it just drops the file right where you are. So, the next time this happens to you—don't let go of the mouse (at least not yet any-way)—simply change directions and drag the file up to the Finder window's title bar and release the mouse button there. Mac OS X will dutifully put your icon right back where it came from—no harm done.

   SELECTED TOO MANY ICONS? USE THIS UN-SELECT SPEED TIP

If you have a number of icons selected in a Finder window, you probably already know you can add more icons by holding the Command key and clicking on them, but if you want to deselect a group of icons, here's a quick way to do it: You still hold the Command key, but this time drag a selection (with your arrow cursor) over the icons you don't want to remain selected. This deselects any icons you don't want to affect.

   SPEED NAVIGATING IN THE SAVE AS SHEET

Want to speed things up by using the keyboard to get around in the Column View in the Save As Sheet? There's just one thing you have to do first—press the Tab key. That removes the highlighting from the name field, and puts the focus on the Column View. Now you can use keyboard shortcuts (like the Arrow keys) to zoom right where you want to be. When you get there, press the Tab key again to highlight the Name field so you can name your file, and then hit the Return key to "make it so!"

QUICK SHUT DOWN

If you want to shut down, and I mean in a hurry (like if you work at Apple and you see Steve Jobs coming down the hall toward your desk and he doesn't look like he's in a terribly good mood), and you have a keyboard with a Power button, just press the button.

   A dialog will appear asking if you want to Shut Down (highlighted), Restart, Sleep, or Cancel (in case Steve takes a sharp turn right outside your office and heads for the restroom). This is a particularly handy tip for people who (a) use PowerBooks or iBooks, or (b) work on the fourth floor at Apple's headquarters.

   Ah—you have an Apple Pro keyboard and it doesn't *have* a Power button? No sweat. The upper right key on the keypad is the Eject key, with a triangle above a bar as its symbol. It's meant for your CD-ROM drive, but press Control-Eject and you get the same shut down dialog. By the way, once the dialog appears, you don't actually have to use the mouse: Typing R(estart), S(leep), or C(ancel) works the same as clicking that button, and hitting Return or Enter activates the highlighted Shut Down button. It's mega quick.

    THE END OF CONTROL-CLICKING IS IN YOUR CONTROL

Tired of Control-clicking? Maybe it's time to buy a two-button mouse. (What!!!! A Mac with a two-button mouse?) I guess Apple figured at some point we'd get tired of Control-clicking, so in Mac OS X if you connect a two-button USB mouse to your Mac, the second button automatically becomes the "Control-click" function (just like a PC's Right-click). From that point on, every time in this book when it tells you to Control-click (like on Application tabs in the Dock), instead you can just Right-click.

FOUND MORE THAN ONE? OPEN 'EM ALL AT ONCE!

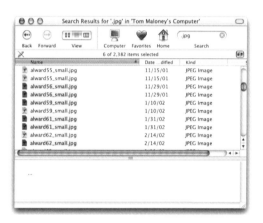

If you're searching for files using Mac OS X's built-in Find command (Command-F), and it turns up more than one "right answer" (in other words, you found four files you want to open, rather than just one), you can open all four at once. Just Command-click on the files you want to open (right within the Search Results window), then press Command-O, and all the files will open, one right after the other.

FIND SPEED TIP: FIND IT AND CLOSE THE RESULTS WINDOW FAST!

If you use Mac OS X's built-in Find function to find a file and open it, you can save yourself time by having the Find function automatically close the Search Results window for you, as soon as your document opens. All you have to do is hold the Option key as you double-click on the file to launch it, and the Search Results window will close immediately, saving you from having to close it manually later.

CAN'T FIND IT? MAYBE YOU NEED TO INDEX

If you're trying to find a file by searching the contents of your files (rather than just by filename) and you can't find a file that you're certain is on your drive, you should probably have Mac OS X re-index your drive. You do this by clicking on the drive you want to be indexed, and then press Command-I to bring up its Info window. Click on the right-facing triangle next to "Content Index" to expand its pane, and then click on the button called "Index Now." You can also do the same thing with a folder—such as your Documents folder perhaps: index it if you're having a hard time finding a file that you're certain is in there.

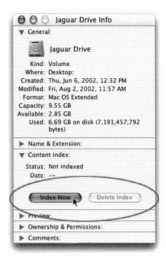

 SPEEDY SEARCHES USING JUST ONE FOLDER

If you find yourself searching a particular folder fairly often (like your Music folder for MP3s or your Documents folder), you can set up the Find function so it just searches in that folder. Here's how: Press Command-F to bring up Find, then from the Search In pop-up menu, choose Specific Places. This brings up a window showing where the Find function will search. Now, back in the Finder, navigate

to the folder you want to have added to this list, and drag-and-drop that folder right into the Find's Specific Places window and that folder will be added to the list. Uncheck any other drives/folders and only the checked folder will be searched, giving you lightning-fast searches.

WHICH APPLICATION MIGHT OPEN THIS FILE?

If you have a file but you don't know which application created it, you can guess. Well, by that I mean you can guess which application might open it, and you can find out almost immediately by simply dragging the icon of the "mystery" document and dropping it on the Dock icon of a program you think might open it. For example, if you have a document that you think might be a graphic (such as a .jpg, .pct, .tif, .eps, etc.) drag-and-drop it on the Dock icon for Photoshop. If Photoshop has a chance in hell of opening it, it will highlight as your icon passes over it (provided, you have Photoshop in your Dock, of course). If it's a text file of any kind, try dragging it to Microsoft Word. Get the idea? Here's another tip: If the app icon doesn't highlight, it probably won't open it, but if you don't believe it (in other words, you think the application is lying to you), you can try to force it to at least try by holding Option-Command and then dropping the document on the application's Dock icon.

   DO YOU WANT ONE WINDOW UP FRONT, OR ALL OF THEM?

Remember how back in the old days of Mac OS 9 and earlier, if you were working in one application and clicked on the window of another open application, all the open windows of that app in the background all popped up front? Well, even if you don't remember, that's the way it worked. Well, in Mac OS X, Apple changed the way windows and apps stack, and now if you're working in an app and click on a document window from another app, just that window comes to front, leaving the rest behind (weird, I know). If that weirds you out, instead of clicking on a document window, just click on that application's icon in the Dock, and all of its windows will be brought to front, just like "the old days."

HAVE MAC OS X LAUNCH YOUR FAVORITE APPS AUTOMATICALLY

If you use the same applications every day (and most people do), you can have Mac OS X open these for you automatically, as soon as you log in. Here's how: Go under the Apple menu (or to the Dock) to System Preferences. In the System Preferences pane, click on the Login Items icon. Click on the Add button, navigate to one of the applications you want to have automatically launched when you log in (if you're the only one who uses your machine, it's probably

already set up to log in for you automatically, so these applications will launch after startup). Choose the application you want, and click the Add button. Repeat for any additional applications. Cool option: You can set it up so the application will launch but then stays hidden from view until you click on it in the Dock. To invoke this way cool feature, click on the "Hide" checkbox next to the application's name when you choose it in the Login Items dialog box.

HOW TO KNOW IF YOU'VE SAVED THAT DOCUMENT

Have you saved the document you're working on? Can't remember? Don't worry, in many cases (depending on the application) Mac OS X remembers for you, and even lets you know it hasn't been saved by placing a black dot in the center of the red "close" button up in the title bar of your document. If you see the dot, it hasn't been saved. If after you've saved the document, you go on to make any other changes (even just typing a word or two, etc.), the dot reappears, telling you changes have been made since the last save. Pretty smart (at least for an operating system).

ONE CLICK TO FIND

If using the simple Search field in a Finder window's Toolbar didn't give you the results you want, you can bring up the full-blown "Find" function fast by simply clicking on the word "Search" right below the Search field.

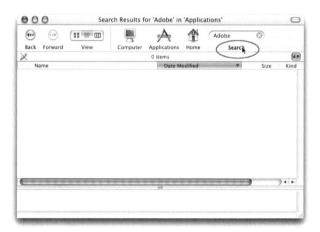

 CLEARING THE SEARCH FIELD

If you're using the Search field in a Finder window's Toolbar, you can quickly clear your last search (so you can type in another). Just click once on the little "x" that appears in a

tiny gray circle on the right side of the Search field, and it immediately clears the Search field and hides the little "x" until you search again.

cool &
the gang

WAY COOL

TIPS

I know, I know, it's supposed to be "Kool & the Gang" (with a "K") not "Cool & the Gang" with a "C." Okay, Mr./Ms. Smarty Pants—you know so much

Cool & the Gang

way cool tips

about the band, which one is "Kool?" The lead singer? Wrong! That's JT. Kool is actually the bass player—the guy who originally formed the band. Okay, now what was their first million-selling single? "Ladies Night?" "Celebration?" "Too Hot?" "Fresh?" Nice try. It was "Jungle Boogie." Gees, I don't know where you got all this attitude, because apparently aside from spelling their name, you really don't know that much about the band. Now, what does all this have to do with Mac OS X? Plenty. For example, let's say you're invited to a party, and the host asks you to prepare an '80s dance mix using iTunes. Well, it's the night of the party, the front door opens and who walks in? That's right—Kool & the Gang (hey, it could happen). You walk up to JT and say "Hey Kool, it's great to meet you," and everybody looks at you like you walked up to Darius Rucker and said "Hi Hootie!" Anyway, here's a "Celebration" of tips that were "too hot" to be contained in any other chapters. (I know—they're lame puns, I don't care—I'm using 'em.)

PUTTING THE DESKTOP IN YOUR DOCK

If you download a lot of files from the Web (MP3s, photos, etc.), then you'll save lots of time by putting your Desktop icon in your Dock. Why? Because if you've got your browser open and you're

downloading files, after you've downloaded just a few, Mac OS X starts stacking them in columns across your desktop. The problem is, you can't get to these newly down-loaded files because your browser window covers them. So you're constantly going to the Finder and hiding your browser so you can access them, right? But by putting the Desktop icon in your Dock, now you can just click on it, and a window opens with all the files on your desktop. Now you can play your MP3s, or trash already unstuffed .sit files. When you're done, just press Command-W to close the Desktop window, then click back on your browser window. This is a *huge* time and frustration saver, but it's one you'll have to try once to appreciate.

   PLAY MP3s FROM THE INFO WINDOW

If you downloaded an MP3 file, you can play it without opening iTunes or any other MP3 player for that matter. Just press Command-I to bring up the file's Info window, then click on the right-facing gray triangle to the left of the word Preview to bring up the Preview pane. A QuickTime-like thin horizontal bar will appear. Press the play button and the song will play from right there, within the Info window.

THE SECRET SCREEN CAPTURE SHORTCUT

Okay, you probably already know the ol' Shift-Command-3 shortcut for taking a screen capture of your entire screen, and you may even know about Shift-Command-4, which gives you a crosshair cursor so you can choose which area of the screen you want to capture. But perhaps the coolest most-secret hidden capture shortcut is Shift-Control-Command-3 (or 4), which instead of creating a file on your desktop, copies the capture into your Clipboard memory, so you can paste it where you want. (I use this to paste screen captures right into Photoshop.)

   SILENCE OF THE BEEPS

If you have a keyboard that has volume controls right on the keyboard (like most PowerBooks), then you're probably used to hearing a little "confirmation" beep each time you press one of these volume controls. If those little beeps get on your nerves (who needs more things beeping at them?), then just hold the Shift key and this will silence the beeps as you press the volume keys.

   PUTTING CLASSIC'S CONTROL PANELS ONE CLICK AWAY

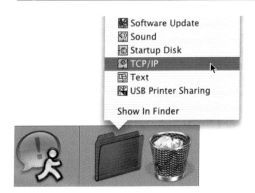

If you use Classic applications a lot, you probably find yourself in the Classic Control Panels from time to time. That can be a pain if you need to get to one while you're working in Mac OS X, because to access the Classic Apple menu, you first have to switch to a Classic app. That is, unless you open the OS 9 System Folder and drag the Control Panels folder onto your Dock where you can access those Control Panels without having to jump over to Classic mode. Better yet—once there, you can Control-click on this folder, and a pop-up list of the Control Panels within will appear, so you can jump right to the individual Control Panel you need.

   DON'T FEEL LIKE OPENING PHOTOSHOP?

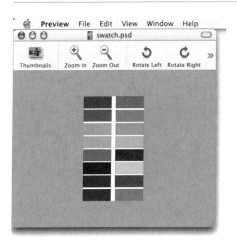

If you need to take a quick look at a Photoshop file, but don't feel like launching Photoshop, just drag the icon to the Preview application icon in the Dock, and Preview will open the Photoshop file. If the Photoshop file is layered, it will even display all visible layers.

DO YOU MISS THE OLD TRASH CAN?

This is one of my favorite tips in the whole book, because I'm a longtime Mac user and darnit, I admit it—I miss having the Trash at the bottom-right corner of my screen. If you miss it there too, here's how to get your own (even though there are five steps, it's absolutely simple to do):

STEP ONE: Go to your desktop and create a new folder by pressing Shift-Command-N.

untitled folder

STEP TWO: Make an alias of this new folder by pressing Command-L, then name this alias folder "Trash" (you can now delete the original folder—you don't need it anymore).

STEP THREE: Click on the alias folder and press Command-I to bring up its Info window. Click on the "Select New Original" button, and the "Fix Alias" dialog box will appear asking you to pick a new original. The original you're going to choose is the Trash, and here's how to do it: In the Go To field at the bottom of the dialog box, type in this: /users/yournamehere/.trash (of course, don't type "yournamehere," instead put your user name in there. If you don't know what it is, look inside your Mac's Users folder and look at what the Home icon is named). Press the Go button and it will find and highlight the Trash file on your drive (it will appear highlighted, but its name will be grayed out). Now, click the Choose button to make that folder become an alias of your Trash. You're almost there.

untitled

Trash

STEP FOUR: Click on the Trash icon in the Dock to open its window. Then press Command-I to open the Trash's Info window. Now press Command-C to copy the Trash icon.

STEP FIVE: Go back to your Trash folder icon on your desktop, click on it, press Command-I to bring up its Info window, then press Command-V to paste the Trash icon over the Folder icon. All that's left to do now is drag your new Trash alias down to the bottom right-hand corner of your screen, and you've done it!

Trash alias

    CREATE ACROBAT PDFs ON THE FLY

By now you're probably familiar with
Adobe's Acrobat technology (and its
Acrobat suite of products), which
enables you to create a file in most any
application and share that file with other
users, on other platforms. Even if they
don't have the same application or the
same fonts, they can see and even print
the document and it will look exactly the
same as it did on your Mac. Well, even if
you don't own Adobe's full Acrobat

application, Mac OS X can build a quick PDF file for you—so you can share your document
with, well...just about anybody on any platform. Here's how: When you're in the application and you're ready to save as a PDF, press Command-P (the standard Print shortcut) and
in the Print dialog box, click on the "Save As PDF" button at the bottom of the window. A
dialog will appear asking you to name your file and decide where to save it. Click Save and
Mac OS X instantly creates the PDF for you. Does that rock, or what? Note: If you're using
Apple's Preview application, it's slightly different—just choose Export from the File menu,
and then in the Save Sheet that appears, choose PDF for Format.

    MAKING SCREEN CAPS OPEN IN ACROBAT

By default, any screen captures you take (using the system's Shift-
Command-3, or -4 shortcut) will create PDF (Portable Document
Format) files that will automatically open in Apple's Preview
application when you double-click on them. If you'd prefer to have
them open in something else (I personally prefer to open PDFs in
Adobe's Acrobat Reader), then do this: Take a screen capture, and
then click on its icon (it should be easy to find, as it's probably
called Picture 1 and is sitting on your desktop). Then, press
Command-I to bring up its Info window. Click the right-facing gray
arrow to the left of the words "Open with:" to expand this pane.
From the "Open with" pop-up menu, look for Acrobat Reader. If
you don't see it, just choose Other, and then navigate to it or any
other application that you may want to use to open screen captures (in this case, I would
navigate to Acrobat Reader), then after you've chosen the app, click the Change All button
in the Open with pane. From now on, all screen captures will now open in Adobe Acrobat
Reader, rather than Preview. Cool, eh?

DIM THE LIGHTS. DRAW THE CURTAINS—IT'S SLIDE SHOW TIME

The next time you're forcing someone to look at digital photos of your recent hernia operation on your Mac, don't open them one by one in Picture Viewer—that's brutal. It's bad enough that you're making them look at the photos of your procedure, you should at least give 'em a show using Mac OS X's built-in slide show projector (okay, it's not a projector in the Bell & Howell sense, but it creates a pretty slick slide show right on your screen). Here's how to create your own, and before

you know it, your friends will see you coming and immediately run for cover:

STEP ONE: Create a new folder and name it appropriately (perhaps something like "Photos nobody but me really cares to see"). Drag your photos of your outpatient procedure into that folder. Go to your Home folder window, and drag this folder of photos into your Pictures folder.

STEP TWO: Go under the Apple menu or to the Dock, under System Preferences, and when the dialog appears, click on the Screen Effects icon. When the Screen Effects panel appears, click on the Screen Effects tab, and in the list of screen effects choices on the left side of the screen, click on the effect named "Pictures Folder."

STEP THREE: On the right side of the dialog, click on the "Configure" button and a Save Sheet-like list of slide show options will appear (including choices for cross-fading between slides, zooming back and forth, cropping slides to fill screen, etc.). Choose your options, and then click the Set Slide folder button above the Display Options to choose which folder within your Pictures folder you want to use for your slide show (in this case, you'd choose the folder named "Photos nobody but me really cares to see"). In a few moments, you'll see a small preview of your slide show right there in the dialog, but if you want "the bigtime full-screen test," press the Test button.

STEP FOUR: Lastly, you'll need to know how to turn this slide show on once you've exited the System Preferences. Click on the Tab for Hot Corners, and you'll see a checkbox in each of the four corners of the screen (well, it's a large icon of your screen). Choose a corner, and then close the System Prefs. When you're ready to start your slide show, just drag your cursor to that corner of your screen and wait just a moment and your slide show will appear. To stop it, just press any key.

   OPENING THE CD TRAY BY MAGIC (ON OLDER MACHINES)

If you're running Mac OS X on an older machine (by older, I mean it's not one of the newer units which have a button for popping out your CD tray right on the keyboard), you may not be out of luck—try holding down the F-12 key for a few seconds (which invokes the Eject CD command), and your keyboard tray should pop out. I say it "should" pop out, because I haven't tried it on every machine with every keyboard, so instead, let's say "I hope it will pop out" or "I feel pretty good about it popping out" or perhaps even "I bet it pops out."

   FORCE QUITTING KEYBOARD SHORTCUT

Need yet another way to force quit a running application (hey, force quitting is all the rage in Mac OS X)? Try the ol' Option-Command-Esc key routine. That brings up a list of applications you can force quit, and by golly your current one is already highlighted and ready to quit. If force quitting is what you really want to do, just click the glowing "Force Quit" button and it'll do its best to bring your application to its knees.

QUICK SET: WARNING BEEP SOUND

Here's a hidden little tip for changing the volume of your alert beep right from the desktop. The pop-down volume control (Menu Extra) on the top right of your Menu Bar controls the overall system volume; but if you hold the Option key, the pop-down slider now controls the volume of just your system's alert "beep."

DIDN'T MEAN TO MOVE IT? SEND IT BACK WHERE IT CAME FROM

Did you just move a folder you didn't mean to move? Worse yet, did you drop a file into a folder and didn't mean to do it? Just Undo it—press Command-Z and the file will return to where it was before you moved it.

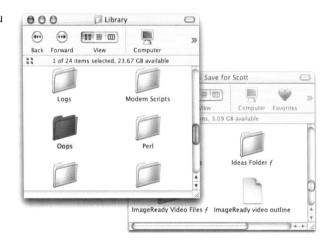

CRANKING THE JAMS BEYOND REASON!

Earlier in this chapter, I showed how you could actually play an MP3 file (or audio file) right from within the Info dialog by choosing Preview from the pop-up menu. Well, the first part of this tip makes that feature more usable, but the second part tears the roof off the sucka (so to speak). First, if you use the Up/Down arrow keys while playing an MP3 file in this fashion, it changes the volume (which is handy, but it isn't the killer part of this tip). The killer part is to add the Shift key, keep pressing the Up Arrow key, and (get this) it actually cranks your volume way past the maximum loudness of your current system setting. Try this once and you'll find yourself "cranking the jams" more often than not!

BUILT-IN TEXT STYLE SHEETS. WHAT???!!!!

This is a pretty cool thing Apple snuck in back in 10.1, and it's been flying under the radar ever since. Sadly, it doesn't work in every application, but it works in apps like Apple's TextEdit and Stickies, and some other Cocoa apps. If you have formatted some type (let's say it's in the font Times New Roman, at 18 point, and it's both Bold and Italic) and you want to apply those same type attributes to another block of text that has completely different font fomatting (let's say the other text is Helvetica 12-point regular), try this: Highlight some of the text that has the format-ting you want and press Option-Command-C. Then, highlight the text that you'd like to have

these attributes (the Helvetica 12-point), and press Option-Command-V. The highlighted text will take on your originally copied font attributes (Times New Roman, 18-point, Bold and Italic)—kind of like a Style Sheet in QuarkXPress, InDesign, or PageMaker. (Note: For Stickies, the shortcut is Command-3 to copy and Command-4 to paste.)

GETTING TIRED OF THAT DESKTOP? SHAKE THINGS UP

If you're getting tired of seeing the same old desktop background (sure you are, you just don't realize it). Maybe it's time to shake things up (which is street slang for "let's have the system put some others up there once in a while to break up the dark, never-ending monotony that is our olive drab, so-called life.") You do this by going under the Apple menu, under System Preferences, and clicking on the Desktop icon. At the bottom of the panel, turn on the checkbox for "Change picture" and then choose how

often the OS should step in and glamourize your otherwise blue-desktopped life. Want to really throw caution to the wind—turn on the Random order checkbox (you rebel!).

  PARANOID PRIVACY TIP

If you're working on some top-secret stuff on your machine (like compiling an internal list of the salaries and bonuses of all top-level Apple executives that you want to post on MacMinute.com), and you don't want anybody (like Steve Jobs perhaps) snooping around your computer if you were to walk away for a moment to get a tasty snack from Cafe Macs, you can password protect Mac OS X's built-in screen saver. That way, once your computer goes to sleep, it will require

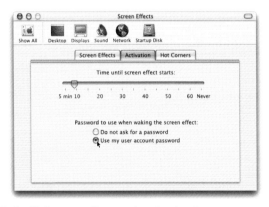

a password to wake it up. To invoke this little "job-saver," go under the Apple menu, to System Preferences, and click on the Screen Effects icon. Click on the Activation tab, and where it says "Password to use when waking the screen effect" click on the button for "Use my user account password." That's it—Steve's locked out. Unless of course, he calls one of his über-engineers who'll hack past your screensaver password protection faster than the Mariah Carey movie *Glitter* went from theatrical release to DVD.

MENUS WITHOUT THE MOUSE

Check this out—you can actually navigate through your menus without turning on the Full Keyboard Access System Preference. Here's how: Just click once on a menu (don't click-and-hold), then just press the Up/Down arrow keys and watch what happens—you can now navigate up and down that menu—and if you press the Left/Right Arrow keys, you can jump to any of the menus in your Menu Bar. By the way, this doesn't work in Classic Mode. (Did I even have to say that?)

   CREATING A COPY OF A WEB GRAPHIC

Want a copy of an image you see on a Web page saved on your hard drive? Just click-and-drag it right from your browser window onto your desktop, and it will appear there momentarily (I'll wait here while you give it a try. Okay, see it there? Great). To open the file, just double-click on it. If it's a JPEG, Picture Viewer will probably rush to open it for you.

GET RID OF THAT ANNOYING FILE EXTENSION DIALOG FAST!

If you've saved a file and later realize it needs to have a three-letter file extension (like .jpg or .gif for the Web), when you go and add those to the file's name, Mac OS X gives you a warning dialog asking you if you're sure you want to make this change. If you

meant to add the extension (and frankly, I'd be surprised if you were adding it to a file by accident. Whoops—my fingers fell on the keys and accidentally added .jpg to my Photoshop image), you can make this dialog disappear just as fast as it appeared by pressing the Esc key as soon as it makes its annoying appearance.

   NAVIGATING IN OPEN/SAVE DIALOGS

Earlier in the book, we looked at how you can navigate through a Finder window using a grabber-like hand. Well, you can pull the same trick when opening or saving a file. To move up or down any Open/Save column that has scroll bars, just press Option-Command and click within the column and your cursor will change to a Hand tool, and you can click-and-drag up or down.

CHANGING YOUR DEFAULT DESKTOP PICTURE

The ubiquitous blue desktop background that is the default for Mac OS X is named "Aqua Blue.jpg" and it's found in the main Library folder, in the folder called Desktop Pictures. Want to create your own default desktop background? Drag this image into Photoshop, erase the blue background, and create the image you want for your desktop background (or drag an existing file into this document). Then, replace the "Aqua Blue.jpg" in your Desktop Pictures folder with this new Photoshop file.

● ● ● **USING PDFs AS DESKTOP BACKGROUNDS**

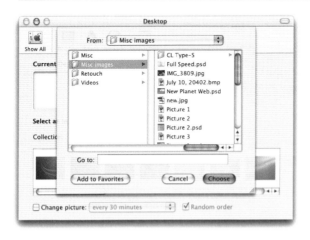

Okay, everybody in the world uses JPEGs and PICT images for their desktop backgrounds, but you— you're a rebel. A free spirit. A "crazy one" (if you will), so you're willing to think outside the box and try a PDF file as your background. Better yet, if you use Adobe Illustrator, open a cool piece of Vector art, save it from within Illustrator as a PDF, then use it for your desktop background by dragging it into the Desktop Well (inside the System Preferences, under Desktop).

QUICK SWITCH TO OS X

You already know about using the Startup Disk panel of System Preferences to choose OS 9 or OS X for your next startup. Well, if you have both OS 9 and OS X on the same disk (or in different partitions on the same disk) you can skip those steps when switching from OS 9 to OS X. Just restart, holding down the "X" key, and you will boot directly into OS X. Very cool. Sorry—it doesn't work going the other way.

   WHAT'S THE SIZE OF THAT GROUP? LET MAC OS X DO THE MATH

Want to know the file size of one icon? No sweat—just press Command-I and check out its size in its Info window, right? What if you want to find out how much space 8 or 9 or even 20 files take up? That's easy too—just Command-click on each file you want added to the total, then press Command-I and the Info window will do the math for you by adding together all the file sizes together and displaying the total.

   IF I COULD TURN BACK THE HANDS OF TIME

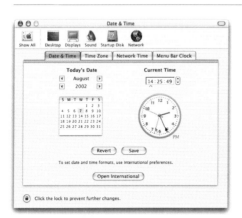

This tip is just for fun, because honestly, it's not tremendously practical, but it looks pretty cool. The next time you're changing the time, using your System Preferences Date & Time panel, and one of your friends or coworkers is watching you, instead of typing in the desired time, just grab the hour and minute hands of the preview clock and move them to set your time. Again, it serves no real purpose, but every time I set my clock like this with someone looking, they're always amazed by it. Unless they're Swiss, of course.

   GETTING FONTS TO LOOK THEIR BEST ON YOUR SCREEN

Mac OS X already does a special brand of font smoothing (a form of anti-aliasing) to make your fonts look crisp and clean on screen. However, you can tweak how it smooths your fonts to give you the best possible look depending on which type of monitor (flat panel, CRT, etc.) you're using with your Mac. To choose which style of font smoothing works best for your monitor, go under the Apple menu, under System Preferences, and click on the General icon. In the General panel, in the bottom section, choose which type of font smoothing you want from the "Font smoothing style" pop-up menu.

144 CHAPTER 8 • Way Cool Tips

Although this is clearly the shortest chapter in the book, it may be the most: (a) fun, (b) cruel, or (c) a delightful combination of the two. (The

Cheap Trick
mac os x pranks

difference between "fun" and "cruel" is the difference between "reading the pranks" and "implementing them.") The original outline for this book didn't have a "pranks" chapter at all, but as I was writing particular tips for the other chapters, I'd sometimes think, "Boy, if you didn't know about this, and somebody who did know it wanted to mess with you, they could pretty much bring your Mac life crashing down around you." I imagined this could create a new brand of Mac heroes—people who would pull these pranks in secret on the machines of unsuspecting coworkers, then show up later to offer to "take a look at the problem," and within a few clicks, it's fixed, winning the respect and admiration of the victim and other office coworkers.

I feel pretty safe in sharing these pranks, because I know you're not the type of person to use or abuse these little gems. Right? Right? Hello…

SOMETHING JUST DOESN'T ADD UP

Annoyance Factor 3: This is more of a "warm-up" prank designed to get your "victim" just a little off balance before you get into the juicier stuff later in this chapter. Go under the Apple menu, under System Preferences, and click on the International icon. In the panel that appears click on the Numbers tab. Inside this panel, under Currency, click on the "After number" button. This moves the dollar symbol ($) after the number (changing $1,200.45 into 1,200.45$). Then, in the Separators section, change the decimal point to "Space" and the Thousands Separator to "Space" (which changes $1,200.45 into 1 200 45$). Again, they may track this down fairly quickly, but then again...

 LOCKING THEM OUT OF THEIR OWN MACHINE

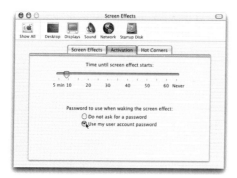

Annoyance Factor 5: This is a good one to pull on someone who is a single user (they're not sharing their machine with other users) and thus they're not used to logging in each day with a user name. Go under the System Preferences, click on the Screen Effects icon, and choose the Activation tab. Set the "Time until screen effect starts" to 5 minutes, but the key thing here is to click on the button called "Use my user account password." That way, when they try to wake from sleep, it will require them to enter their user password—if they can even remember what it is. Ahh, it's the simple things in life.

JAMMING THE DOCK

Annoyance Factor 10: This is just one of those things that make people crazy, because without getting your hands dirty, there's really no quick way to undo the damage, and it takes a long time and a lot of keystrokes to get things back to the way they were. Start by looking through the victim's hard drive until you find a folder with lots of items (any folder with 50 or more items qualifies, but think "the more the merrier!"). Press Command-A to select all, and drag them all to the right side of the Dock. Repeat this in as many folders as you like, until your victim has hundreds (if not thousands) of items in their Dock. (A good place to start looking for folders with a lot of items is inside their Home folder, inside the Library folder, inside the Caches folder, inside the iPhoto Cache folder. There's at least 126 items right off the bat—dying to be dragged to some poor soul's Dock, at three or four times in a row.) Not only will this make their Dock microscopic in size, there's only one way (short of some serious under-the-hood system tweaks) to get these items back out of their Dock—dragging them out one-by-one. A full reinstall is probably faster. This is something you should probably save for your last day at your current job, for obvious reasons.

   THE CASE OF THE MISSING HARD DRIVE

Annoyance Factor 7: It's the simple things in life that make it worth living. Like removing someone's hard disk icon from the desktop. To do this, Go to Finder Preferences, and under "Show these items on the Desktop" uncheck the checkbox for "Hard Disks." The next time they start up, their hard drive won't appear on their desktop, and their subsequent freak-out will begin.

   THE WONDERFUL WORLD OF INTERNATIONAL RELATIONS

Annoyance Factor 8: This one only has an 8 as its annoyance factor because if the victim has really used the OS for a while, they might (I say might) be able to figure it out, but not without a little educated guessing and plenty of wasted time. For most folks, though, it will be a 9.5, worthy of a total reinstall. That's because you're going to change the entire language the OS is displayed in to a foreign language. Go under the System Preferences, click on the International icon,

and choose the Languages tab. To change languages systemwide, drag one of the listed languages to the top of the list. Easy, for sure, and perhaps a bit obvious, but here's where you really toast 'em—click on the Edit button, and the languages that are displayed in the Languages tab are listed with a checkbox by each. Uncheck all but the new language you just chose in the previous screen. That way, even if they fumble their way to the Languages list, English won't be in the list—only the language you chose. I like to use Nederlands, because it changes a simple English menu command like "Allow Hyphenation" to "Sta woordfabreking toe." How could that be a bad thing? (Tip for you: the System Preference for International is now named "Landinstellingen"). Changing to Japanese is fun too, and much harder for your victim to repair because figuring out the Japanese menu command for "System Preferences" is quite a bit more challenging. As are the commands, "International," "Languages," and "Edit," too!

SHIFT-BEEP. OPTION-BEEP. COMMAND-BEEP. BEEP-BEEP!

Annoyance Factor 7: Would it drive you crazy if suddenly every time you pressed Shift, Option, Command, or Control, it would make an annoying beep and then giant icons (that represent those modifier keys) appear on the upper-right side of your desktop? Sure it would. Wouldn't it be funny if that suddenly happened to a friend's or coworker's machine? Sure it would. Go under their System Preferences, click on the Universal Access icon, click on the Keyboard tab, and turn on Sticky Keys. Will they know where to go to turn the beeping and giant icons off? I doubt it. One of two things will happen: (1) They learn to live with it, or (2) they'll do a reinstall.

   SAYING GOOD-BYE TO MAC OS X

Annoyance Factor 5: Go under the System Preferences, under Startup Disk and change their system to start up using Mac OS 9.2, and then shut down their machine. Next time they start up their Mac, it will skip Mac OS X altogether and open in System 9.2 instead. Restarting their system won't help; it'll boot into 9.2 again and again until they figure out how to change their startup disk to 10 using 9.2's Control Panels. Or—if they know to hold down the X key while starting up. This will boot in OS X. You gotta love that.

  TAKING AWAY THEIR PRIVILEGES

Annoyance Factor 2-8: depending on whether or not they're on a network: This is a great prank to play on a single user who's not connected to a network, because they won't have any experience with setting folder privileges. Go to their Documents folder, click on it, and press Command-I to bring up the Info window. Click on the right-facing gray triangle to the left of "Ownership & Permission" to bring up that pane. From the Owner/Access pop-up menu, choose Read Only. This makes the contents of their Document folder (where documents they create are saved by default) pretty much locked. They can't drag files into it, they can't delete files within it, they can't even save an open document into their own Documents folder (how ironic is that?). They can basically only read files within it, and that's about it. When they try to do most anything else, they'll get a nasty warning informing them that they don't have privileges to do what they're trying to do. People seem to really get annoyed with that. If you're really in a bad mood, maybe set the Owner/Access permission to No Access, or Write only.

   UNEXPLAINED LAUNCH MYSTERIES

Annoyance Factor 6: If you know which applications your victim uses most, the fun is about to begin. Click on a document from one of those applications. For example, let's say that they use Microsoft Word quite a bit. Look on their drive for a Word file (a document with the Word document logo on it). Click on one of those documents, and then press Command-I to bring up the file's Info. In the Info window, click on the right-facing gray triangle to the left of "Open with" to reveal the "Open with" pane. When that pane appears, from the Open with pop-up menu choose "Other," and then from the resulting dialog box, choose a different application. Try something like Adobe Illustrator 10 (if they've got it), or if not, you can try something as tame as Apple's Mail application (which comes with OS X). Then, click on the "Change All" button, and finally, close the window. The next time they double-click a Word file, it won't launch Word—instead it will launch and open in Illustrator (or Mail). Annoying? You bet. Try changing any Photoshop files to open in Preview or, worse yet, have them open in Graphic Converter. There's just no limit to the fun.

APPLICATION ICON MADNESS

Annoyance Factor 9: Imagine if you clicked on an application and instead of launching the application, it just opened an empty Finder window. This would get mighty frustrating, wouldn't it? This type of thing would basically bring a person's work to a halt, wouldn't it? Sound good? Here's what to do:

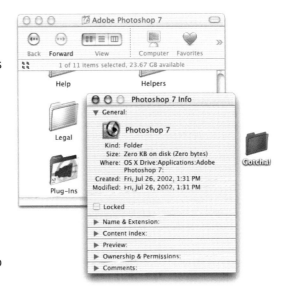

STEP ONE: Create a new blank folder on the Desktop and name it "Gotcha!".

STEP TWO: Go to their Applications folder, open a folder for one of their major applications (something like Photoshop), and click on the Photoshop application icon. Press Command-I, and when the Info window opens, press Command-C to copy the Photoshop icon.

STEP THREE: Now drag just the Photoshop application icon into your Gotcha! folder.

STEP FOUR: Go back to their Applications folder, and open their Photoshop folder. Press Shift-Command-N to create a new blank folder within their Photoshop folder.

STEP FIVE: Press Command-I. When the Info window opens, press Command-V to paste the Photoshop application icon onto this blank folder. Rename this folder Photoshop.

STEP SIX: Then, go to the Dock and remove the Photoshop icon (if it's there). Repeat this process for the rest of their major apps, and every time they launch an app, all they'll get is an empty Finder window.

Once they're in tears, you can lead them to the Gotcha! folder—for a small fee.

IF I COULD TURN BACK TIME

Annoyance Factor 6: I left this simple, yet deceptively effective prank till last because it can really screw up people's lives, even beyond reinstalling their OS. Go to the System Preferences and click on the Date & Time icon. Simply click back one year in the calendar, and for at least a day or so, every e-mail they send to anyone (their boss, a big client, etc.) will wind up at the bottom of the recipient's inbox, making them think the victim never sent the e-

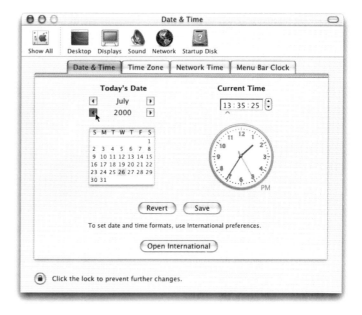

mail at all. This is the kind of thing that gets people fired, loses big accounts, and makes otherwise happy couples break up, so use this only on people who pull Mac OS pranks on you with an annoyance factor of 6 or higher. Serves 'em right.

takin'
care of
business

BUSINESS
APPLICATIONS

I know what you're thinking. Does Address Book really count as a business application? I mean, if you're using it for storing personal contacts (like

Takin' Care of Business

business apps that come with mac os x

your bookie, your pharmacist, your bail bondsman, etc.), then it's really not a business application, true. But, if you gave your bookie some Darvocet you got from your pharmacist to pay off a bad debt, but then he got busted and looked to you to bail him out (which is a surprisingly common turn of events), then it's all business, baby. Yeah, what about TextEdit? Hey, the thing's nearly Microsoft Word 5.1, gimme a break— total business. Unless of course, you wind up using TextEdit to methodically detail your plans for a multi-million dollar gold heist. Then it's a fun caper-planning application. Well, until you're caught, and your bookie has to come down to the jailhouse and bail you out, and by that time he's had to pawn your iBook to raise your bail money, and now all you have is a spiral bound notebook and a piece of chalk. Address Book doesn't seem so bad now, does it, Bunky?

   TextEdit: **YOUR FREE WORD PROCESSING APPLICATION**

If you think you need to go out and buy a word processor for business letters and basic word-processing tasks—save your money—Apple gave you a pretty slick word processor and it's already installed on your drive. It's called TextEdit, and although it looks a bit like SimpleText (Apple's bare bones text editor from Mac OS 9) when you first launch it, it has real word-

processing capabilities that SimpleText can only dream about (that is, if text editing applications actually dream—and there's considerable debate about that. At the very least, they dream in black-and-white. Get it? Okay, sorry about that one). You find TextEdit in your Applications folder. (Mine now lives in my Dock and I use it daily because it launches faster than a greased pig.)

   TextEdit: **HOW DOES MY LETTER FIT ON A PAGE?**

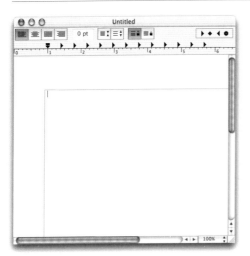

To see TextEdit's page boundaries, press Shift-Command-W (the shortcut for the "Wrap to Page" command) and the page margins will appear on screen. Another thing that will make TextEdit behave more like the word processor it really is, is to go under the Format menu and choose Allow Hyphenation, so when a word extends to the page edge, it gets automatically hyphenated and split by syllable to the next line, like you'd expect in a stand-alone word processor.

TextEdit: COPYING FONT FORMATS

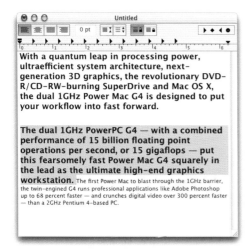

I mentioned this elsewhere in the book, but I thought it bore repeating here because this is such a cool tip and TextEdit totally supports it (not all Mac OS X apps do). If you've got a block of text formatted just the way you want it (font, type style, size, color, etc.), you can copy just that formatting (not the words themselves) by highlighting the text and pressing Option-Command-C. Then, to apply that copied formatting to another block of text that's formatted with different font styles, sizes, etc., just highlight this other text and press Option-Command-V. That text will now have the same font formatting as your original text. Big, big timesaver.

TextEdit: COPYING PARAGRAPH FORMATS

Another typography tool usually found in page layout applications and full-powered word processors is paragraph styles. Like the font formatting copying we talked about in the previous tip, in this instance you'll be copying the paragraph formatting (first line indents, justification, tabs, etc.). To do this, highlight part of the paragraph that has the formatting you want, then press Control-Command-C to copy that formatting. Then switch to another paragraph, highlight that paragraph and press Control-Command-V to paste that formatting onto this paragraph.

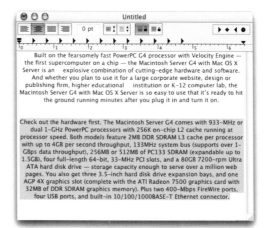

TextEdit: **ADJUSTING THE SPACE BETWEEN LETTERS**

Kerning is the act of adjusting the space between letters. (When it's called "kerning" that usually refers to adjusting the space between just two letters. If you're adjusting more than two letters at once, it's usually called "tracking.") At standard text sizes like 10, 11, and 12, you don't normally worry about kerning, but when you start creating display-sized type (like 72-point type), sometimes wide gaps appear between letters.

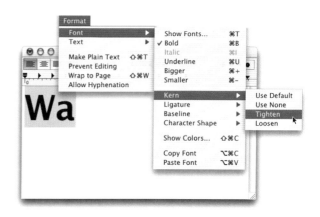

(The space between a 72-point capital W and the small letter "a" is a perfect example.) To tighten the space between letters, highlight the letters then go under the Format menu, under Font and Kern, and choose Tighten. This is a very slight adjustment, so you'll probably have to run it more than once (okay, probably more than five or six times). To Loosen the space, choose Loosen as many times as you need.

 TextEdit: **FORMATTING YOUR FONTS**

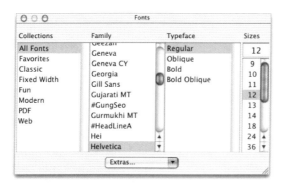

TextEdit gives you fairly robust control over your font formatting. Press Command-T to bring up the Fonts dialog. You can choose the font family, typeface style (bold, italic, etc.), and point size. But even more controls are found under the Format menu under Fonts. You'll see everything from controls for colorizing your text, to advanced text formatting features you're more likely to find in high-end page layout applications like kerning, ligatures, and baseline shift.

TextEdit: MISS SIMPLETEXT? BRING IT BACK

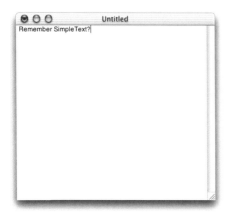

If you miss the clean wide-open "rulerless" look of SimpleText (from the Mac OS 9 era), you can have TextEdit mimic that look. Simply launch TextEdit, and then press Command-R (Show Ruler) to hide the Ruler, buttons, and entry fields that make TextEdit look more like the word processor it really is, and less like its country cousin—the wonderfully bland SimpleText many people grew to love (because of its speed and sheer simplicity).

TextEdit: POP-UP SPELL CHECKING

If you want to spell check your TextEdit document, save yourself a trip to the Menu Bar. Simply Control-click right within your document and a pop-up menu will appear where you can take control of the spell-checking process. This works particularly well if you have a word in question—just highlight that word, control-click within it, and the proper spelling (if misspelled) will appear in the pop-up menu.

By the way—if you prefer to have the Spell Checker check as you type, and flag misspelled words as soon as they're created, go under the TextEdit preferences, and under Editing, turn on "Check Spelling As You Type."

TextEdit: ZOOMING IN

Want a closer look at your work in TextEdit? Click on the pop-up menu at the bottom-right corner of your document window and choose the level of magnification you'd like—up to 1600% and down to as little as a 10% page view.

   TextEdit: **GETTING GRAPHICS INTO TEXTEDIT**

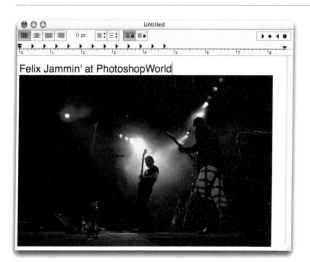

Probably the fastest way to get graphics into TextEdit (it supports JPEG, PICT, TIFF, and GIF) is to drag-and-drop the graphics files right from a Finder window (or your desktop) into your TextEdit document. You can also copy and paste between applications such as Photoshop and TextEdit.

TextEdit: **SWAPPING FILES WITH WORD USERS**

Sharing files with someone using
Microsoft Word? No sweat—TextEdit
supports the Rich Text Format (.rtf) so
just ask your Word-using friend to save
his file in Rich Text Format directly from
Word. You'll not only be able to read
and edit his document, you'll be able to
send it back to him in a format that he'll
be able to read, and it will hold any
formatting changes you applied to the
document while in TextEdit.

 TextEdit: **OPENING WEB PAGES**

Believe it or not, TextEdit also
lets you open and view Web
pages. Now, I'm not just talking
about viewing the HTML source
code that most text editors (even
SimpleText) can do—I'm talking
about opening a Web page and
having it look like a Web page
when you're viewing it online in
your browser—complete with
graphics (I know, it's wild).

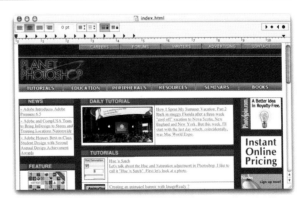

    TextEdit: **ALWAYS WRAP TO PAGE**

Want to see those page margins every time you create a new document? Go under the TextEdit menu and choose Preferences. In the TextEdit preferences, under New Document Attributes, check the box marked "Wrap to Page" and from then on, every new page will automatically display the page margins.

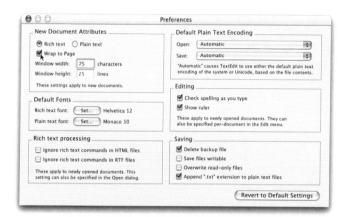

    Stickies: **GETTING BACK THAT CLOSED NOTE**

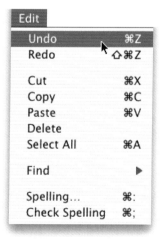

Have you ever accidentally closed the wrong note, or closed a note you didn't mean to? If so, as long as you think fast, you may get that note back—just press Command-Z (Undo) before you do anything else and it will reopen the note you just closed.

Stickies: POP-UP SPELL CHECKING

Want to have
Stickies spell-
check for you as
you type? Just
Control-click on
the Sticky you
want to check,
and from the
pop-up menu
that appears,
under Spelling,
choose "Check

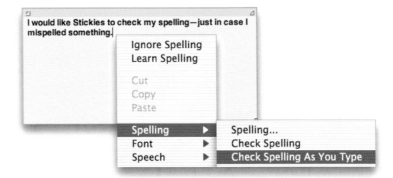

Spelling As You Type." Then, when you misspell a word, it will immediately be flagged
(underlined with red dots). You can then Control-click on the flagged word, and Stickies
will give you a suggested spelling, and if you like, you can replace the flagged word with
the properly spelled word from the pop-up menu.

   ## Stickies: FROM STICKY TO TEXTEDIT IN ONE CLICK

If you get carried
away in a Sticky
and you wind up
writing more than
you expected,
you can instantly
convert your
Sticky Note into a
TextEdit docu-
ment by selecting
all your text and
then going under

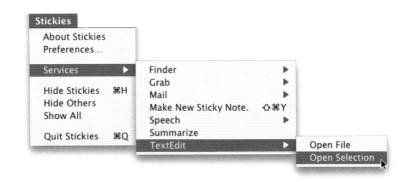

the Stickies menu, under Services, under TextEdit, and choosing Open Selection. This
will immediately launch TextEdit and open a new document with the contents of your
Sticky within it. You can now save your file in TextEdit format and use all of TextEdit's
features as if your file had been created in TextEdit to begin with.

Stickies: SETTING FONT, STYLE, AND SIZE DEFAULTS

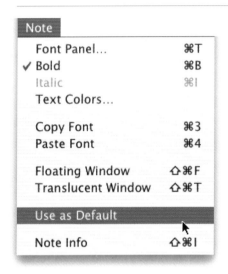

If you have a favorite font and size you like to use for your Stickies, you can quickly change the defaults so every new Sticky will use your favorites. Just open a new Sticky, press Command-T to bring up the Font Panel, and set your font, type style, and size, just the way you like it. Then, go under the Note menu and choose Use as Default. Now, when you open a new Sticky, it will use your new custom default settings.

Stickies: YES, I WANT TO CLOSE THAT NOTE

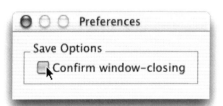

Remember how in previous versions of Stickies, every time you went to close a note, you got a scary-sounding warning dialog asking if you're sure you want to close the note? Well, guess what—you still get that warning (or at least a version of it, asking you if you want to save the note)—but at least now you can turn it off. Go under the Stickies menu, under Preferences, and there's only one thing you can do in there— turn the save warning off.

Stickies: **TURN YOUR SELECTION INTO A STICKY**

If you've selected some text in a Mac OS X application such as TextEdit (a phone number, Web address, etc.), you can turn that selected text into a Sticky in one click. Just go under the TextEdit menu, under Services, and choose Make New Sticky Note. Stickies

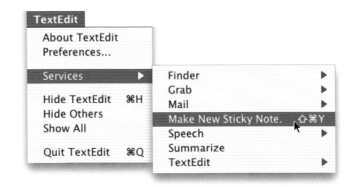

will launch and open a new note with your selected text. The keyboard shortcut for this automation is Shift-Command-Y.

   Stickies: **THE ONE PLACE WINDOW SHADE STILL LIVES**

In Mac OS X Apple did away with the popular Window Shade feature that appeared in previous versions of the OS, where you could double-click on a window's title bar and it would roll up like a window shade, leaving just the title bar visible. But in Stickies, a Window Shade feature still exists—just double-click the Sticky's title bar (or press Command-M) and the current Sticky rolls up—just like a window shade.

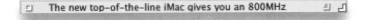

The new top-of-the-line iMac gives you an 800MHz

CHAPTER 10 • Business Apps   **167**

   Stickies: **QUICK ACCESS TO SPELL CHECKER**

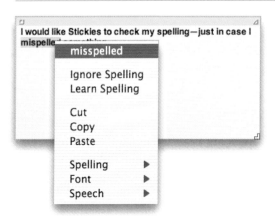

If you're working in Stickies and you're not sure if you've spelled a word correctly, just Control-click on the word, and a pop-up menu will appear. At the top of this menu will be choices for what it believes is the proper spelling of that word (if it's actually misspelled and it recognizes the word in the first place). If you agree, just move your cursor over that word, release you mouse button, and your misspelled word will be replaced. Mighty handy.

   Stickies: **KEEPING YOUR NOTE UP FRONT**

You probably already know how frustrating it can be if you have to toggle back and forth between an open Sticky and another application (let's say you're copying some figures from Stickies into Microsoft Excel). Well, now the toggling is finally over: just press Shift-Command-F (the command for "Floating Window"), and this will make your current Sticky note float above your current application. That way, you can clearly see your note while working in another application (like Excel) because it'll be floating above it.

Try this once, and you'll be using it daily. Provided, of course, that you use Stickies daily. And use your Macintosh daily. And that you use Stickies with another application daily. And that you bathe daily. (I just threw that last one in as a subtle personal hygiene reminder. See, I care.)

Stickies: **SEE-THROUGH NOTES**

One of my favorite Jaguar Sticky features is the ability to make a Sticky translucent. Just click on a Sticky and press Shift-Command-T (Translucent Window). Then you can see right through your sticky to the items behind it. This is really handy if you want to see items in Finder windows that would normally be covered by any open Stickies. To turn off the transparency (pardon me, "translucency"), just press the shortcut again.

   Stickies: **SAVING YOUR TEXT COLORS**

You've been able to colorize text in Stickies since at least Mac OS 10.1, but did you know that you can save your favorite colors and apply them with just one click? (Obviously, I'm hoping you didn't or it really kills this tip). To do so, just highlight a word, then go under the Note menu and choose Text Colors. When the Colors dialog appears, choose the color you'd like. Then, click-and-hold in the horizontal color bar up top (where the color you've created is displayed), and a tiny square will appear under your cursor. Just drag-and-drop this square on one of the white square boxes at the bottom of the Colors dialog. This saves that color for future use, so when you want it, all you have to do is click once on that square (no more messing with the color wheel). This is a great place to save commonly used colors like red, solid black, white, etc.

Stickies: PUTTING STICKIES IN MOTION

Actually, this tip really should be called
"Motion in Stickies" because believe it
or not you can put a QuickTime movie
into a Sticky. Just locate the QuickTime
movie you want (don't open the movie,
just find it on your drive), and then open
Stickies. Drag out your Sticky's window
so it's big enough to accommodate the
physical dimensions of your movie, and
then drag-and-drop your movie right
from the Finder window (or desktop)
into your Sticky note. You'll get a dialog
asking if you want to actually Copy it
there, or just place an Alias of it there.
Choose Copy, and within a few moments

it will appear within your Sticky with a standard embedded-style QuickTime player bar
beneath it. Click the Play button, and your QuickTime movie will play from right
within your Sticky note. Why would you want to do this? I have no idea.

Stickies: JOT DOWN A QUICK NOTE ANYTIME

Working in the Finder and need to jot
something down real quick? Just press
Shift-Command-Y and Stickies will instantly launch and open a new Sticky for
you. It's superfast and pretty darn handy.

Font Panel: BETTER THAN KEYCAPS: FINDING WHERE THE © AND THE ™ LIVE

Since nearly the beginning of Mac-dom, when you wanted to find out which key combination produced a font's special characters (stuff like ©, ™, £, ¢, ‰, ƒ, etc.), you used a utility (originally known as Desk Accessories) called "Keycaps." Sadly, more than a decade later, this incredibly lame utility still ships with the Mac OS, but at long last a better implementation is upon us as part of the Font Panel. To access, and even input, special characters, press Command-T to bring up the Font Panel (available in Mac

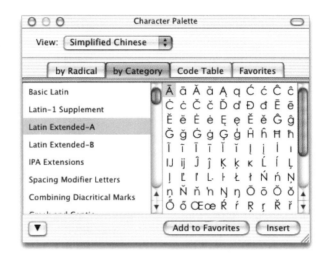

OS X apps like Mail, TextEdit, Stickies, etc.), and from the pop-down menu at the bottom of the panel choose Show Characters. When the Character Palette appears, click on the "By Category" tab. The left column shows a list of special character categories, and the right column shows the individual characters in each category. To get one of these characters into your text document, just click on the character and press the Insert button in the bottom-right corner of the dialog. If you find yourself using the same special characters over and over (like ©, ™, etc.) you can add these to your Favorites list, and access them from the Favorites tab in the Character Palette. To see which fonts contain certain characters (they don't all share the same special characters) expand the Character Palette by clicking on the down-facing arrow on the bottom-left side of the palette. This brings up another panel where you can choose different fonts. You can also ask that this list shows only fonts that support the character you've got highlighted.

   Font Panel: NAVIGATING THE FONT PANEL VIA KEYBOARD

You don't have to click font-by-font anymore in the Font Panel (like back in the old days of 10.1, etc.). Now, you can move up/down the font list using the Up/Down Arrow keys on your keyboard. Even better, for full speed navigation in the Font Panel, you can Tab through the different fields using (you guessed it) the Tab key. Between the tabbing and the Up/Down Arrow keys shortcuts, using the Font Panel is almost palatable (sorry 'bout that one).

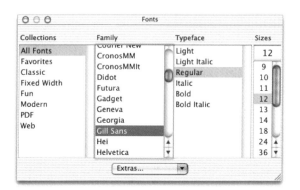

   Font Panel: ACCESS SPECIAL CHARACTERS FROM THE MENU BAR

If you need a quick special character (such as é, or °, or ˆ) but don't know which keyboard combination you need to create it, you can have the Character Palette (a list of every character) added to your Menu bar. Here's how: Go under the Apple menu, and choose System Preferences. Click on the International

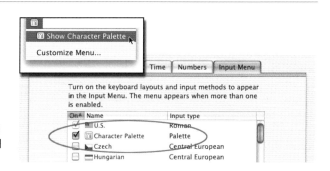

icon. When its pane appears, click on the Input Menu tab, and in the list of Characters, turn the checkbox on for "Character Palette." This adds a little icon to the right of the Help icon in the Finder, where you can quickly choose "Character Palette" without going through the Font Panel.

Font Panel: **SEEING YOUR FONTS BEFORE YOU USE THEM**

Apple has heard your plaintive cries, and finally they've included a preview of your fonts so you can actually see what they look like before you decide which one to use. You access this new wonder of modern science in any application that uses Mac OS X's built-in Font Panel (apps such as TextEdit, Stickies, Mail, etc.). Press Command-T to bring up the Font Panel. When it appears, click on the pop-up menu at the bottom of the panel and choose Show Preview. A font preview pane will appear at the top

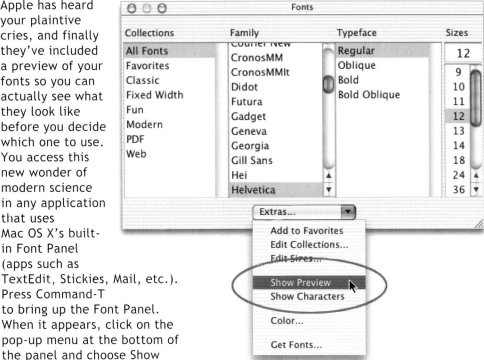

of the dialog box, and as you click on different fonts, their preview will appear in that pane. It works for both type style and font sizes as well.

Mail: **FITTING MORE IN YOUR MAIL DRAWER**

If you have a lot of mailboxes, your Mail Drawer can get pretty crowded. If that happens, just Control-click within the Drawer and choose Use Small Mailbox Icons from the pop-up menu that appears. These smaller icons will create much more room, enabling you to fit more in your Drawer (so to speak).

   Mail: **QUICKLY BACKING UP YOUR E-MAILS**

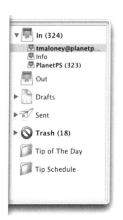

If you want to archive (or backup) your e-mails (I often back mine up to a FireWire drive just in case things go south), here's an easy way: Make your Mail Drawer visible, then click the little gray right-facing triangle to the left of your on Inbox icon. This expands the Inbox downward listing your e-mail accounts. Just click on the e-mail address you want to archive, and either drag it right out onto to the desktop, or if the hard drive or server you want to backup to is visible, drag it right there for an instant backup.

   Mail: **CONTROLLING YOUR MAIL SEARCH**

If you're searching for a particular piece of mail (aren't we all? I'm still searching for that one from Publishers' Clearing House) you can either expand or narrow your search by choosing search options. You access these by clicking on the tiny down-facing triangle just to the right of the Magnifying Glass icon within the Search field. A pop-down menu will appear where you can choose how wide (or narrow) a search you want initiate.

   Mail: **QUICK ACCESS TO MAIL COMMANDS**

If your Mail app is running, but you're working in another application, you can save time by accessing a number of Mail's commands right from the Dock by just Control-clicking on Mail's Dock icon. A pop-up list of commands will appear, including shortcuts for checking your mail and composing new messages.

Mail: **YOU'VE GOT MAIL? LOOK IN THE DOCK**

You'll see another example of how cool Mac OS X's Dock is the first time you use the built-in Mail program (simply called "Mail"). As mail comes in, the number of messages you have in your Inbox are displayed right on the Mail icon itself in the Dock.

   Mail: **CUSTOMIZE MAIL'S TOOLBAR**

This is another place you can customize the Toolbar, and probably one of the most useful because most users will only take advantage of a few tools, so why clutter the Toolbar with tools you won't ever use, right? As usual, Control-clicking on the Toolbar brings up a contextual menu where you can choose which size you want for your icons, and whether you want them displayed with icons and text, or just icons or just text (and which size you want for both). If you Command-click on the white pill-shaped button in the upper-right corner of the title bar, you'll step through the various Toolbar icon/ text configurations. Hold Option-Command and click the same button, and the all-important Customize Toolbar sheet will appear.

Mail: **HOW TO MAKE YOUR MAIL DRAWER SWITCH SIDES**

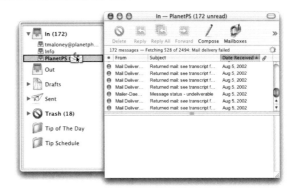

You know how the Mail Drawer (the little panel that holds your In, Out, Drafts, etc.) sticks out from the right side of your Mail window? Well, here's a little tip on getting it to "switch sides." In your Inbox, click on a mail message and simply drag it off the left side of the Mail window. The little panel will immediately jump to that left side to "catch" your e-mail (providing, of course, that there's enough room on your screen for it to pop out on the left side. If you have your mail window butted up against the left side of your monitor, it may not have room to pop out. So if you drag the message out and it doesn't pop out, drag your window to the right until there's enough room for it). Best of all, from now on your Mail Drawer will appear on the left side. If you decide later you want to switch back to the right side, just drag an e-mail message off the right side, and the drawer will jump over to that side to catch it.

   Mail: **QUICK WAY TO ADD WORDS TO YOUR DICTIONARY**

If you're typing a message in Mail and run across a word that should be in your Spell Checker's dictionary (such as your name, your company's name, etc.), you can quickly add it to your Mail dictionary (that way, it recognizes the name in the future, instead of flagging it as misspelled). Here's how: When you come to a word you want added to your dictionary (such as the name "Scott," which seemingly should be in every dictionary, but sadly is not), Control-click on the word and choose "Learn Spelling" from the pop-up menu. Now it's added, and it will no longer be flagged as not recognized (unless you misspell it).

   Sherlock 3: **STEP THRU SHERLOCK'S TOOLBAR VIEWS**

Sherlock has a new job in Jaguar—just Web searches (hard drive searches are now relegated to the "Find" command using the shortcut Command-F). Although this has changed, it shares many of the same Toolbar controls as other Mac OS X apps. For example, if you Command-click on the white pill-shaped button in the upper-right corner of Sherlock's title bar, you'll get another Icon/Text view that's smaller than the default Toolbar view (which is large icons and large text). Click once, you'll get smaller icons. Click again—icons with no text, then smaller icons with no text, then just text, and then just really small text. To hide the Toolbar altogether, click once on the white pill-shaped button in the upper-right corner of Sherlock's title bar, and it will hide itself from view. Want to customize its Toolbar? Just Control-click anywhere within the Toolbar itself and choose Customize Toolbar.

Sherlock 3: TARGETING CHANNELS THE FAST WAY

Know which Sherlock 3 channel you need next? Don't waste time—jump right to it by Control-clicking on Sherlock's icon in the Dock. A pop-up list of Channels will appear and you can jump right to the one you need fast. (Note: If you quit Sherlock after your last search, this won't work—it has to be running, but it doesn't have to be the active application, meaning, you could be running Adobe InDesign, and jump right to the Sherlock channel you want directly from the Dock.)

Sherlock 3: OPENING MORE THAN ONE SITE

If Sherlock has done a Web search for you, you can check out more than one site simultaneously as long as your Web browser is set up to open a new URL in a new window. Start by clicking on one site in Sherlock's results window, then Command-click on any other site to add it to your list. While still holding the Command key, double-click on either one to have both open in browser windows. If you want to open a contiguous list of site results, click on the top result, hold the Shift key, then double-click on the last result and all the sites in between will be opened as well.

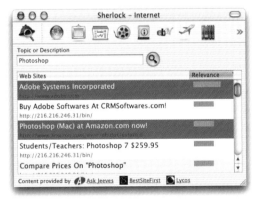

   Sherlock 3: **MOVING THE NAME COLUMN. WHAT??!!**

I know what you're
thinking—moving the
Name column—it can't
be done. Mac OS X just
doesn't let you do
that. Oh sure, you can
click, hold, and drag
to reorder columns in
any Finder window,
and many other

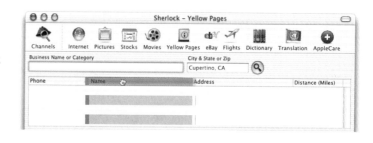

applications, but as a rule Mac OS X never lets you move the Name column out of its
safe, comfy home at "first column on the left." Well, that age-old rule is broken in
Sherlock where you're actually allowed to click-and-drag directly on the first column
and drag it to a different location. Do it once, just because you can.

   Sherlock 3: **SAVE THAT SITE FOR LATER**

If Sherlock finds a site that
you think you might want to
save for later (kind of like a
"Favorite"), just click on it
(in the results window) and
drag it right to your desktop. It will create a double-
clickable file that you can
use to get back to that
exact Web page any time.

Sherlock 3: **REMOVING CHANNELS**

If there's a Channel that you just don't ever see yourself using, you can Control-click on it and choose "Remove Item" from the pop-up menu that appears.

   Sherlock 3: **PERFORMING MULTIPLE SEARCHES**

Let's say that while you're checking on the details of an arriving flight, you also need to find out what time *Austin Powers Goldmember* is playing at the local AMC, and you need to be simultaneously searching for "Think Different" posters on eBay. How do you pull off this "miracle of multiple searches?" It's easier than you'd think. Just start one search in motion, then choose New from the File menu to bring up another search while the previous one's still chunkin' away. I told you it was easy.

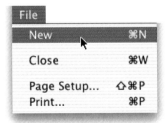

Address Book: **GET TO THEIR SITE FAST!**

Scott Kelby
KW Media

Note:

If you have a person's or company's Web site listed within their contact info, you can get to it fast (without typing any info) by just clicking on the word "Home Page" in their contact info, and choosing "Go to Web Site" from the pop-up menu that appears. It will automatically launch your Web browser and take you right there.

   Address Book: **WAS IT KAL-IB-RA OR KAL-EEB-BRA?**

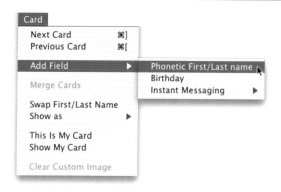

If you enter a new contact and you're concerned that when you call them again, perhaps months from now, you won't remember how their name is pronounced, Address Book can help. Just go under the Card menu, under Add Field, and choose "Phonetic First/Last name." This adds a tiny field right above your contact's name where you can enter the phonetic spelling of their name, so when you do call them back you sound like a genius (or at least, someone with a good memory).

Address Book: SENIOR-SIZED PHONE NUMBERS

Okay, the phone numbers in the contact window are pretty small, but don't sweat it, you can make the numbers so large that senior citizens who are standing a good 15 to 20 feet from their monitors could make them out. Just click-and-hold directly on the name of the field for the number you want to read (Work, Home, Mobile, etc.) and choose "Large Type" from the pop-up menu that appears. The menu item should really read "Huge, gigantic, billboard-like type" because it plasters the number in giant letters across your entire screen. (Try it on an Apple Cinema Display—it's stunning.) To make the huge numbers go away, just click once on them and they disappear, back into a giant cave.

Address Book: SENDING E-MAILS FROM ADDRESS BOOK

Okay, technically you're not sending the e-mail from directly within Address Book, because you're using Address Book and Mail together. Just click directly on the title for the contact's e-mail field (mine is "work" but yours could be different—just look for a field that's followed by an e-mail address) and choose Send E-mail from the pop-up list. It launches Mail and puts an e-mail address in the New Message "To" field for you auto-matically. All you have to do now is type the message and click Send.

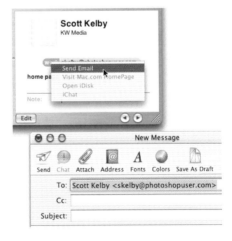

   Address Book: **GETTING vCARDS IN FAST**

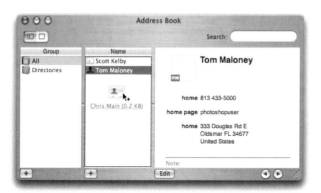

vCards (Virtual Business Cards) are getting so popular that they now have an "industry standard" format, and luckily, Address Book not only supports but makes it easy for you to enter vCards. If you're e-mailed a vCard, just drag-and-drop it right into the Address Book window and Address Book will automatically format the information into a contact for you.

   Address Book: **SKIP THE http:// AND THE www. Even .com**

When adding a Home Page to a contact in your Address Book, if he has a simple home page (such as Apple.com, MacDesignOnline.com, or Adobe.com) you can usually skip the entire process of entering http://www. before the address. In fact, you can even skip the .com part. For example, if you wanted to add my personal Web site to a contact, you could just enter "scottkelby" instead of the longer http:// www.scottkelby.com and it would still work. This works with most simple Web addresses, but once you start adding slashes and .html at the end, you may have to at least add the www. at the beginning.

work ⇕ Phone
mobile ⇕ Phone

work ⇕ Email

home page scottkelby

home ⇕ AIM (AIM)

Address Book: **MAKING YOUR OWN vCARD**

I know, I know, you want to be all trendy and hip, so here's how to make your own vCard. (Note: The first step in being trendy and hip is not to use the 1970's word "hip.") Here's how: First, set up your own personal card the way you want it, then go under the Card menu and choose "This Is My Card." This will change the icon for your personal contact to a silhouette of a person, rather than a square photo icon, letting you know which card is "your card." If

you've got a lot of contacts and want to get to your card fast, choose "Show My Card" from the Card menu. If you want to e-mail your card to somebody (to show you're trendy and that other thing), first choose Show My Card from the Card menu, then go under the File menu and choose Export vCards. Save your vCard file (I save mine right to my desktop) then send it as an attachment to any Mail file. You can also drag-and-drop your card's silhouette icon right from Address Book straight into a New Message window in Apple's Mail app. Or if you're using iChat, you can send your vCard to someone you're chatting with by going under the iChat File menu and choosing Send File.

   Address Book: **QUICK ACCESS FROM MAIL**

If you don't want to keep Address Book in your Dock all the time, you can still access it quickly when you're working in Mac OS X's Mail app. Just go under Mail's Window menu and choose Address Book and it will immediately launch and come to front.

Address Book: **GET DIRECTIONS TO THEIR OFFICE**

Now this is really cool—you can have Address Book automatically get a map and local directions to your contact's physical address. Just click on their address field (not the address itself, the field title before it) and choose "Map Of" from the pop-up menu that appears. It will quickly go online and get a map and directions to their location for you. Seriously, how cool is that!!!!

   Address Book: **MERGING TWO RECORDS**

If you have two contacts for the same person (it happens more than you'd think—at least to me), you can have Address Book merge the two into one contact. First, press Command-1 to make sure your mode is set to Card and Columns view. Then use the Search field (in the upper-right corner) to find the two redundant contacts. Then, in the Name column, click on the first contact. Hold the Shift key and click on the second to select them both. Then, go under the Card menu and choose Merge Cards, and the two shall become one (like the way I switched writing styles there? "The two shall become one." Hey, if nothing else, I'm versatile). If any of the information is redundant (two of the same phone numbers, etc.), just press Command-L to go into Edit mode, highlight the duplicate info, and press Delete. When you leave Edit mode, not only will the duplicate info be gone, the duplicate field will also be deleted.

Address Book: **GETTING GRAPHICS INTO YOUR ADDRESS BOOK**

Don't let the fact that the little square photo swatch in your contact info window is so, well...little and square. It's more powerful than it looks as it supports almost any graphic format that you throw at it, including even PDF files. Just drag-and-drop a photo right on that tiny square and chances are it'll

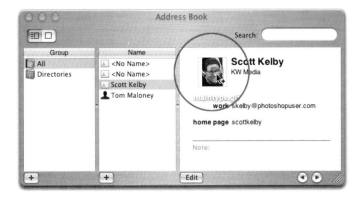

accommodate it (meaning, it'll accept it, and then summarily size it down to fit in its tiny little square).

    iChat: **QUICK WAY TO CUSTOMIZE YOUR BACKGROUND**

Want to put a background photo behind your Chat window in iChat? Just drag-and-drop the photo you'd like as a background right into your message window and it will appear behind your text. If the photo is smaller than the window, the photo will tile (repeat) automatically, just as in a Web browser. To delete it (if it's too busy—like the one shown here) go under the Edit menu and choose Clear Background.

   iChat: **VIEW QUICK CHANGE**

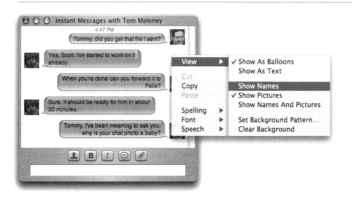

Want to view just text, just photos, both at the same time, or toggle back and forth? Just Control-click right within your message window (where the bubbles appear) and a pop-up menu will appear, and under the View submenu you can choose how you'd like your chat messages displayed.

   iChat: **A BUBBLE OF A DIFFERENT COLOR**

Don't like the default color of your "dialog bubble?" You can change it by going under the iChat menu, and choosing Preferences. When the Preferences window appears, click on the Messages icon and in that pane, choose your desired color from the "My balloon color" pop-up menu. You can also change the color of incoming chat balloons there.

iChat: **PUTTING LIVE LINKS INTO YOUR CHAT**

Want to be able to have the person you're chatting with click on a Web link directly from your chat? It's easy: just enter your text: for example, "You gotta check out this wild new site." Highlight the words "new site" then press Command-K to bring up the Hyperlink window. When it appears, type in the full Web address (e.g., http://www.scottkelby.com) and click OK. That part of your text will now appear as a live clickable link in your message window.

iChat: **GETTING YOUR MESSAGES ONCE YOU'VE QUIT ICHAT**

One of the coolest things about iChat is that you don't have to have it up and running to get instant messages. Just set your status as Available (from the iChat Status menu up in the right side of your Menu Bar) and you'll be able to get messages, and even check to see if people in your Buddy list are available. Best of all, you can set your own personal preferences for how you'd like iChat to let you know you've got an instant message. This is accomplished before you quit iChat, by going under the

iChat menu and choosing Preferences. Click on the Actions icon, and when the pane appears, under Event, choose "New Message Received," then if you like, click the "Speak text" checkbox and your Mac will verbally tell you you've got a message. If you're afraid it won't get your attention, click on the checkbox for "Bounce icon in the Dock." If that's still not enough notification, click the checkbox for "Send repetitive 110-volt electric shocks via keyboard." (Okay, that last one isn't really in iChat, but don't ya think it should be?)

jukebox hero

iTUNES TIPS

Okay, why does iTunes get its own entire chapter, when applications like iDVD, iMovie, and iPhoto are all covered in the same chapter? Well,

Jukebox Hero

iTunes tips

Bunky, there's more than just one reason, and like many lists in life, we'll start with #1: Everybody digs music (even bad people), and everybody loves iTunes (probably even Bill Gates). But iDVD and iMovie have a much smaller audience. For example, if you don't have a digital video camcorder, you probably don't use iMovie, in which case, you probably don't use iDVD either. With iPhoto, if you're not shooting digital photos, you're probably not using iPhoto (though you could), so again, it's not a ubiquitous thing like music. Reason #2: I use iTunes a lot, and I've got so many really cool iTunes tips that they take up an entire chapter. But perhaps the real reason is (#3) after watching iTunes' built-in visual effects for a few hours one day, in a sudden moment of total clarity, I realized that it had become my master, and it told me it needed its own space. Then it asked me to sell my car and give it the proceeds. Yes, master.

GROOVIN' ON THE METERS

When you're playing a song in iTunes, the name of the current song is displayed in the status display at the top center of the iTunes window. In the left center of this status display is a  tiny gray circle with a right-facing triangle in the center. Click on this tiny button, and the name of the song is replaced by a digital EQ meter. Having the EQ meters displayed is important because...uh...it's important because...uh.... Okay, they're not really important, but they look cool, and that should be reason enough to display them in appropriate social situations.

   ## WHERE DID THAT TUNE COME FROM?

Want to know the name of the album the current song came from? Click once directly on the song's name in the status display and the album's name will appear in its place (provided that  the album's name is included with your audio file, in the Tags section of the iTunes info palette).

TIME WON'T LET ME WAIT

By default, the status display shows you the Elapsed Time of the current song (if you've played 30 seconds of your song, it displays 0:30). However, if you'd prefer it to show Remaining Time

(if you've played 30 seconds of a 3-minute song, it displays 2:30) then click directly on the Elapsed Time display and it will switch to Remaining Time. Click again, and it will show the Total Time of the entire song.

   STOP THE SONG INFO-OVERLOAD

The song list window gives you so much info, sometimes it seems a bit overwhelming (especially if you're new to iTunes). But you don't have to live with this "information overload," because you can tell iTunes which fields you want visible by pressing Command-J to bring up its View Options. When the View Options pane appears, make sure only the fields you want visible have a checkmark by them (for example, I show only Song, Time, and Artist in my song list).

   HOW TO PLAY DJ BY BROWSING

iTunes has a slick built-in song-
sorting tool that lets you find songs
by artist, by album, by genre, and
more. So if you're in the mood for
nothing but Blink 182, you can have
your Song list display just their
tunes. Once you've done that, if
you just want to hear their songs
from a particular album, you can
do that too. Or, in a broader sense,
if you want to hear just jazz songs,
you can have only the songs
that you've tagged as "jazz" appear
in the song list. You do this by first

clicking on the Library button (in the Source list), then the Browse button will appear
(on the top right of the iTunes window.) It looks like an eye. When you click it, rather
than giving you a long scrolling list view of all the songs in your library, it gives you
something more like the column view of a Finder window, with different category
panes sorted by info you've entered (or was embedded) in your music files.

   SORTING BY GENRE

Besides the ability to sort by
artist's name and album, if you've
tagged songs by their genre (jazz,
rock, speed metal, etc.) you can
use Genre as a sorting field when
using iTunes' Browse feature, but
it doesn't display genre info by
default—you have to turn it on by
going under the iTunes menu,
under Preferences, in the General
tab, and clicking on the checkbox
for "Show genre when browsing."

I SHALL CALL IT...MINI-TUNES

If you don't need all the bells and whistles that iTunes offers gobbling up your screen real estate, you can request a much more compact version of the iTunes interface that I call "Mini-tunes" (as a personal tribute to Austin Powers' Dr. Evil). You do this by clicking once on the Zoom control button (the green one) in the upper-left corner of the iTunes window. Clicking the green Zoom control button shrinks the iTunes interface down to just a horizontal bar, with your song list and source lists hidden; and all that's left are some tiny basic controls (Play, Fast Forward, Rewind), a mini status display, and a tiny volume slider. If you think "less is more," Mini-tunes is for you.

   SMALLER THAN MINI—IT'S MICRO-TUNES

If you've tried the "Mini-tunes" tip above, but still think it's too big, you can take things a step further and create the smallest iTunes interface known to man. I call it "Micro-tunes." To get there, start by creating Mini-tunes (clicking on the green Zoom control button) and then drag the bottom right-hand corner of the Mini-tunes window to the left. This hides the small status display and leaves only the Rewind, Play, and Fast Forward buttons. If you feel that it still takes up too much space, seriously—it's time to buy a bigger monitor.

   HOW TO EDIT JUST ONE FIELD

If you don't want to enter scads of song info, and you only want to edit one item (like the band's name, song title, etc.), you don't need to go to the Tags dialog—you can just click on the song you want to edit, then click once right on the field you want to edit in the Song list window. The name will become highlighted and

you can edit it right there. Press the Return key when you're done.

   "GOTCHAS" WHEN REARRANGING SONGS

Rearranging the order in which your songs play is easy—just click on the song and drag it to the order you want it to appear—but there are three little catches (gotchas!) that might trip you up: (1) You have to be in a Playlist—you can't change their order in the main Library window. (2) Once you're in a Playlist (rather

than the Library), to be able to rearrange their order by dragging, you must have your Playlist sorted by track number (rather than by song, artist, album, etc.). To sort by track number, just click at the very top of the first column from the left (it's the only blank field header), and then you can drag songs into whichever order you'd like. (3) The third "gotcha" is that you can't do any of this if you have the Shuffle (random play) button turned on, so turn that off before you begin sorting.

TREAT THE SONG WINDOW LIKE A FINDER WINDOW

You can pretty much think of the Song window like a Finder window, because they play by a lot of the same rules: you can stretch the window; you can change the order of the columns (except for the Name column—just like a Finder window); clicking on a column header sorts by that

field (by default, columns sort from A—Z, first to last, top to bottom, etc.—clicking the little arrow in the column header reverses the sort order [Z—A, last to first, etc.]); you change column width by clicking and dragging between headers, etc.

 WHICH SONG IS PLAYING, RIGHT NOW?

To have iTunes highlight the song that's playing right now, just press Command-L.

CRANK IT UP/TURN IT DOWN

If you like, you can adjust iTunes' volume control from the keyboard: press Command-Up Arrow to crank it, or Command-Down Arrow when the neighbors bang on the wall.

Press Option-Command-Down Arrow to mute iTunes if the cops arrive, and press Command-H to hide your stash before you answer the door (kidding. Kind of).

 GETTING GEEKY WITH YOUR PLAY LIST

If you really want to put on a propeller beanie and have an iTunes geek-fest, go under the File menu and choose Export Song List. This exports a tab-delineated text file of your entire iTunes Library and Playlists that you can open in your favorite spreadsheet (or database), with all the song info sorted into fields. If you do this immediately after watching a *Star Trek TNG* repeat, a "Sad Social Life" extraction team is immediately dispatched to your home and they forcibly take you to the nearest rave.

TO AUTOPLAY, OR WAIT TILL THE MOOD STRIKES

What happens when you have iTunes open and you insert an audio CD? Well, actually you can decide yourself by pressing Command-Y to bring up iTunes Preferences. Click on the General icon, and in the middle of the pane is a pop-up menu where you can choose how inserted CDs are handled. It's called "On CD Insert," and you can choose from "Show Songs" (which does just that—no audio), "Begin Playing," "Import Songs" (in which case it imports all songs that have a checkmark by them), and "Import

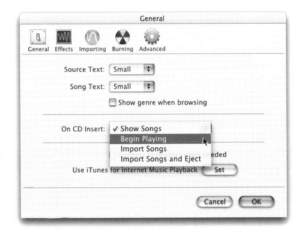

Songs and Eject" (if you're importing a collection of songs from different audio CDs and you want to keep things moving).

   ITUNES FONT SIZING

If the font in the iTunes song list appears too small to you, you can increase the font size by going under the iTunes menu, under Preferences, and clicking on the General icon. In the General Preferences pane, choose "Large" from the Song Text pop-up menu.

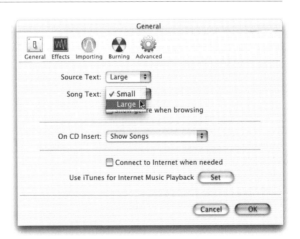

   THE PSYCHEDELIC BUTTON

If you're using iTunes and want to see what life was like for your parents when they were young, press Command-T (or click on the center button on the bottom right of the iTunes window). This turns on iTunes' "Visual Effects"—a sync'd-to-music on-screen display that you'd expect to see projected behind bands like "Cream" and "Jefferson Airplane" during concerts back when people smoked anything that wasn't tied down. These Visual Effects make an LSD trip look relatively mild in comparison (at least, that's what my older brother Jeff says, and he should know). Personally, I

like this psychedelic blast-from-the-past, and sometimes I turn it on simply as a form of personal punishment. But as best as I can tell, the reason this mind-bending visual display is included in iTunes is that at some point, Apple must figure that all Mac users will grab a giant party bong and subsequently want to then (a) stare at some freaky colors for long periods of time, or (b) call Pizza Hut delivery. So far, I've done the "b" part quite a number of times, but I still haven't tried the "a" part. However, if I stare at those visuals long enough, if nothing else, it makes me want to burn my draft card.

   EXPAND YOUR PSYCHODELIA

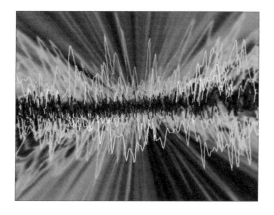

Watching the psychedelic visuals from within the iTunes window is somewhat interesting, but if you really want to get the full mushroom-induced effect, press Command-T, then Command-F, and the effect then takes over your entire screen (and perhaps your entire life).

SELLOUT TO THE GIANT CORPORATIONS

Want to really "mess" with people's heads while they're sucked into the endless vortex of iTunes' psychedelic visuals? Just press the letter "b" while it's turned on and the corporate logo of a giant Fortune 500 company will appear in the center of the visuals and stay there, reminding you that the world is really run by giant corporations and we're powerless to do anything but send them more money and follow their orders. (Okay, pressing "b" really

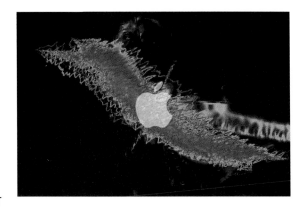

just brings up a white Apple logo center screen, but it sounds much more Orwellian to call it the "corporate logo of a giant Fortune 500 company.")

   ## PRETEND THE VISUAL EFFECTS MATTER

Let's pretend for a moment that these cool Visual Effects are important. If they were, they'd need a set of options to control various aspects of their playback, right? Well, sadly, there *are* options for these Visual Effects— and when they're running within the iTunes window, their Options button appears where the old "Browse" button used to be (in the upper-right corner of the window). They probably figure you don't need the Browse button

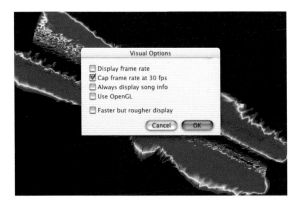

because if you're watching the visuals, you're probably too stoned to start sorting your music files, right? (Kidding. Just a joke, etc.). These options include adjusting the playback frame rate and displaying the frame rate—you know, critical stuff like that.

   DUDE, WHO DID THIS SONG AGAIN?

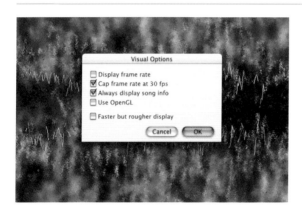

Want to see not only the Visual Effects but also the song name and artist that you're zoning out to? They appear onscreen for a few moments when you first start the Visual Effects, but then they fade away. If you're busy ordering/eating your munchies and can't remember who did the song, or even its name (this is quite common) once the visuals are running, click on the Options button and in the Visual Options turn on the checkbox for "Always display song Info."

   HELP FOR THE VISUALLY CHALLENGED

If you're really serious about iTunes' Visual Effects (perhaps you're a dealer or own a head shop), you might as well learn how to make this puppy really jump through some hoops. While the Visual Effects are running, press "?" (the Question Mark key) on your keyboard to bring up "Basic Visualizer Help"—a list of one-button controls for various other features you can control. I know what you're thinking, "If it says 'Basic help,' then somewhere there must be an 'Advanced help,' right? Right!" Just press the "?" button again, and another screen listing more one-button controls will appear.

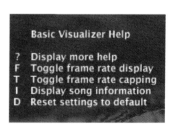

CONTROLLING YOUR EXPERIENCE

Are the colors you see during your Visual Effects experience displeasing you? Is it, in effect, creating a "bad trip?" If so, the next time you're running the Visual Effects, try mashing a few keys. Depending on which keys you press, the color combinations and effects change in real time, while they're happening on screen. For example, if you press the letter "z" it steps you through different color combinations, but better yet—it displays the names of these color schemes on screen. Seeing what the Apple engineers named these color schemes gives an eerie sense of credibility to my "drug-related" gag comments. For example, one color scheme is called "Electric Acid." Another is called "Sunchemicals From a Queen Bee." Somebody call the cops! If you press the letter "q," it changes the wireframe lines that dance to your music. Pressing the letter "a" changes something (I know it's changing, because I see its name changing in the display, but I've yet to figure out quite what it is; but I know after watching it for just a short time, I get a craving for a bag of Cheetos™).

   SAVING YOUR EXPERIENCE

If you use the letters in the previous tip to create your own custom Visual Effects and you come across just the right combination to induce a momentary total loss of equilibrium, you might want to save that combination for future use (perhaps, as a party trick at Rick James' house). Just hold the Shift key and choose a number key where you want to save your custom preset (you can save up to 10 presets, using the numbers 0 through 9). Then, when you want to play "We All Fall Down," just press Shift and the number where you saved it, and that visual will appear onscreen (e.g., Shift-2).

GETTING PLUGGED INTO VISUAL EFFECTS

If you're totally sucked into to the whole Visual Effects thing (I know I joke about it, but it's really pretty cool), there are people out there creating their own iTunes visuals and you can download them from the Web (many are free) and import them into your copy of iTunes. Go to your Home folder and open your Library folder. Inside your Library folder open the iTunes folder and there you'll find a folder called "iTunes Plug-ins." Drop your downloaded Visual Effects plug-ins in here, and then relaunch iTunes.

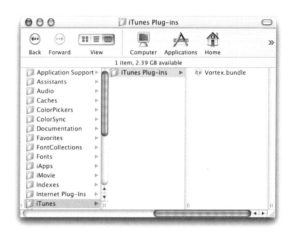

These new Visual Effects plug-ins will now appear at the bottom of your Visuals menu. Now it's time to sit back, turn on the Visuals, and fire up a fatty (again, just a joke).

   THE SECRET REPEAT BUTTON

At the bottom-left side of the iTunes window is the repeat button (it's the third icon from the left). Click once to turn it on, and after iTunes plays your current song list, it starts over and plays it again. However, if you want to hear just one song repeated over and over and over (like a song from the Backstreet Boys

perhaps), click the repeat button a second time and it will then repeat the current song over and over (a little "1" will appear on the button's icon to let you know you're now in "loop land"). I know what you're thinking. Shouldn't this have been in the Mac OS X Pranks chapter? Probably.

TAGGIN' YOUR TUNES

All of the background info for your iTunes music is stored in the Song Information pane. If you download MP3s from the Web, you already know how often song names, artists, and album information is partially or totally wrong (and like this book, they're rife with typos). You can edit these "tags" by clicking on a song in your list and pressing Command-I and clicking on the "Tags" tab. There you can type in the right name (if necessary) and any other supporting info you want access to (artist, album title, genre, CD track number, and your own personal comments).

  AUTO-TAG—YOU'RE IT!

If you're not the type to go in and enter all the tag info manually, you can have iTunes automatically go the Web, research the song info (at the CDDB Internet audio database), and enter it into the Song Information Tags' field for you (how cool is *that?*). There are only two catches: (1) It only works when you're "ripping" songs from an audio CD in your Mac's CD drive, and (2) of course, you have to have an active Internet connection. To set up iTunes to do this automatic search, press Command-Y to bring up iTunes Preferences, click on the General icon at the top, and then click on the checkbox for "Connect to Internet When Needed." If you don't want this feature turned on all the time, when you need to look up CD info, just choose "Get CD Track Names" from the Advanced menu and it'll do its Internet thing.

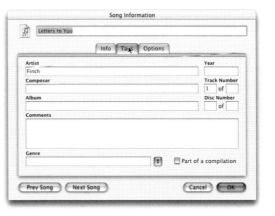

 SAVING YOUR OWN CUSTOM EQ SETTINGS

iTunes has a built-in graphic equalizer (EQ) for adjusting the audio frequency (the tone quality) of your music to get the best quality sound from your speakers. This is particularly important to PowerBook and iBook users whose computers have such tiny little speakers that they possess a flat tone quality enjoyed only by desert squirrels. To bring up the iTunes EQ, press Command-2. You can adjust the sliders manually (bass sliders on the left, midrange in the middle, and highs on the right) or use the built-in presets from the pop-up menu. If you've come up with a custom EQ setting that you want to save for future use, just choose "Make Preset" from the top of the built-in presets pop-up menu. It lets you name your preset, and then your named custom preset is added to the pop-up menu alphabetically.

 ONE-CLICK ON, ONE-CLICK OFF

As I'm sure you already know, in the Song list, only the songs that have a checkmark by them will play in your Playlist (the same thing goes for importing [ripping] songs from an audio CD—only checked songs get ripped). But if you hold the Command key and click on any of the checkmarks, iTunes instantly marks all the songs for you. Command-click again and it unchecks them all.

CONTROLLING ITUNES FROM THE DOCK

I covered this in the chapter on using the Dock, but since you might have turned right to this chapter, I wanted to make sure you didn't miss one of the most convenient iTunes features—the ability to control iTunes while it's minimized to the Dock. Just Control-click on its icon in the Dock and a pop-up list of controls (including the name and artist of the current song) will appear, so you can start, stop, and change iTunes songs without having to bring iTunes to front.

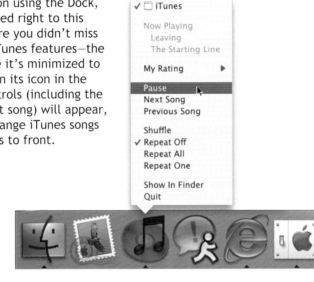

   RUN ITUNES FROM THE DOCK

If you're using Apple's iTunes to sort, organize, and play your jams (I mean, your tasteful musical selections), once it's running, you can minimize it to the Dock because you won't have to open iTunes every time you want to change tunes. Just Control-click on the iTunes icon and a pop-up list of iTunes playback controls appears, including Pause, Next Song, and Previous Song, among others. Heck, it even tells you the title and artist of the song currently playing.

WORKING WITH SONGS THE FAST WAY

If you Control-click on any song in the iTunes Song window, a pop-up menu will appear giving you access to a host of popular commands.

BALANCING YOUR VOLUME

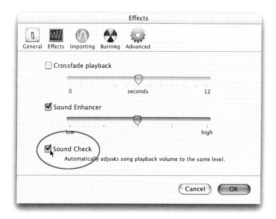

Have you ever had a situation (and I'll bet you have) where you set the volume to just the right level while playing one song, but another song comes on and is either way too loud, or it's too soft? Luckily, iTunes 3 lets you balance the volume between songs with a simple preference setting: just press Command-Y to bring up iTunes preferences, then click on the Effects icon. When the Effects pane appears, turn on the checkbox for "Sound Check," which according to the dialog "Automatically adjusts song playback volume to the same level."

SHORTCUT FOR CREATING SMART PLAYLISTS

Clicking on the Plus Sign button at the bottom-left corner of the iTunes window lets you create new Playlists, but if you hold the Option key, you'll notice that the button changes to a "gear" icon, giving you a quick way to create a Smart Playlist instead.

   BROWSING OUTSIDE THE LIBRARY

In previous versions of iTunes, you could only use the Browser (which lets you sort by Artist or Album) in the Library. Thankfully, in iTunes 3 you can now browse in Playlists as well. Just click on the Playlist and then press Command-B, and the Browser will appear above your song list.

  SUPER FAST COLUMN VIEWS

The quickest way to choose which columns you want visible in the Song list window is to Control-click on any of the headers (such as Song Name, Time, Artist, etc.), and a pop-up list will appear of all the different columns available for viewing. Just check the ones you want displayed.

   A PERFECTLY SIZED ITUNES WINDOW

Wouldn't it be nice if you could have iTunes resize itself to the perfect size— with no extra empty space at the bottom of your Song list, and just wide enough to show the columns you've chosen to be visible. Well, it can (I know, it's not much of a surprise after that lead in). Just Option-click on the green Zoom button (in the upper-left corner of the iTunes window), and it will resize to "the perfect size" (i.e., if your current Playlist has only six songs, then the player window will be only six songs deep).

SKIP THE DYNAMIC RESIZING FOR MORE SPEED

iTunes 3 gives you dynamic window resizing (meaning that everything happens in real time—you drag the bottom-right corner to resize the window and the contents of the window, including lists, search fields, info windows, etc. all resize while you drag). It looks cool, but it isn't super fast. If you feel the need for speed, instead of just dragging that right corner to resize, hold Command and just the outline

of the window will resize (like a "ghost outline"), and when you release, only then will the window's elements be resized, which is much, much faster.

   OPEN ANY PLAYLIST IN ITS OWN WINDOW

If you'd like to have multiple Playlists open at one time, or if you'd just like to have your Playlist open in a separate window, double-click directly on the Playlist's tiny icon (rather than single-clicking its name as usual).

  LIKE THIS SONG? RATE IT FROM THE DOCK

If you're playing a song and decide you want to add or change its rating (how much you like it based on a one- to five-star ranking system), just Control-click on the iTunes icon in the Dock and under My Rating, choose your rating. It doesn't get much easier or faster than that!

   LISTENING TO SONGS WITHOUT COPYING THEM

By default, when you drag an audio file from your desktop (or other Finder window) and

drop it into iTunes, it copies that entire file onto your hard drive. However, if you just want to play the song without making a permanent copy on your drive (maybe it's an MP3 on a CD, on a server, or on a removable FireWire drive), just hold the Option key before you drag. That way, it just points to the original audio file (like an alias) rather than copying it.

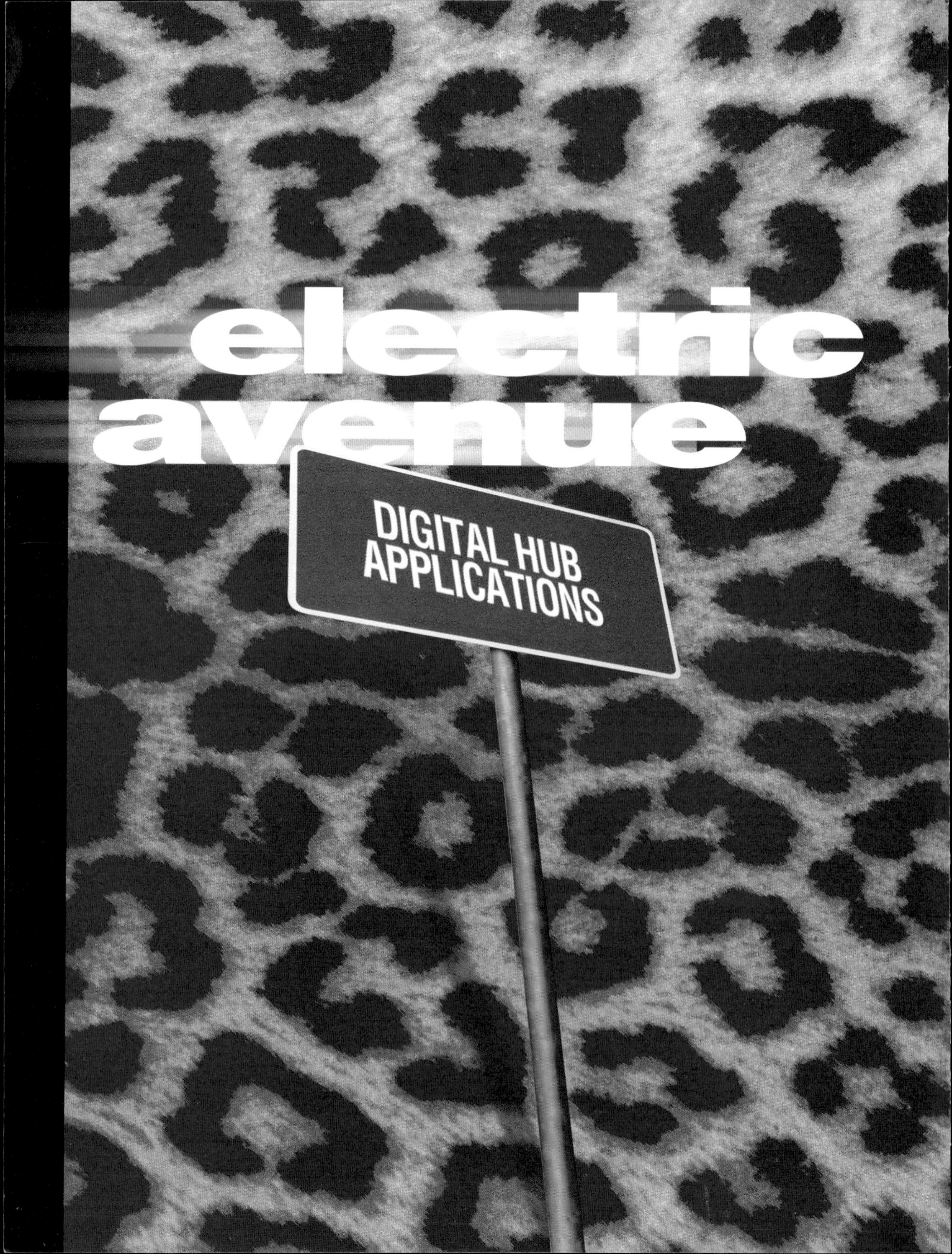
electric
avenue
DIGITAL HUB
APPLICATIONS

When you hear the word "multimedia," what does it really mean? Isn't "multimedia" one of those buzz words that are now so

Electric Avenue

digital hub apps that come with mac os x

"mid-'90s" that they belong with other lame mid-'90s terms like "Information Super Highway" and "Cyberspace?" Absolutely. When I think of the word "multimedia," I think of someone using a slide projector and a cassette player. (Say it to yourself, "Get ready for my multimedia presentation!" It just sounds so 1996.) That's why I chose to use Apple's way cooler made-up term "Digital Hub" for this chapter. Wait a minute? Isn't iTunes (which selfishly has its own separate chapter) considered one of the "Digital Hub" applications? Well…yes. So, if you want to pretend, just for the sake of this exercise, that the iTunes chapter and this Digital Hub chapter are really just one big chapter, that's perfectly fine by me. Yes, but couldn't you lump the two chapters together and use the all-encompassing term "Multimedia Applications" as a chapter head? No. Were you even listening at the beginning of this chapter intro?

   iMovie 2: **THE TRICK TO SETTING IN/OUT POINTS**

If you've ever tried to access the Video Crop Markers under the Playhead in the Monitor, you already know how frustrating that can be—unless you know this tip— just Shift-click directly on the Playhead at its current location and the Crop Markers will immediately appear under the Monitor's scrubber bar.

   iMovie 2: **MOVING CROP MARKERS WITH PRECISION**

Once you have Crop Markers in place, you can be very precise on their placement by using the Arrow keys on your keyboard to position them right where you want them.

iMovie 2: GETTING RID OF THE CROP MARKERS

What happens if you get the Crop Markers in place, and then change your mind—you don't want to crop after all? Just click once in the Monitor window right on your image area, and the Crop Markers will disappear.

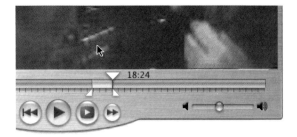

iMovie 2: LET IMOVIE ADD UP THEIR RUNNING TIMES

If you want to quickly find out the running time for two or more clips, iMovie 2 will tell you—just Shift-click on the clips in the Timeline Viewer (or the Clip Viewer), and their combined running time will immediately be displayed in the title bar of the Timeline/Clip Viewer (in that little space just above the clips where it normally displays the title of the selected clip.) It will now read "Multiple" followed by the combined running time of all your selected clips.

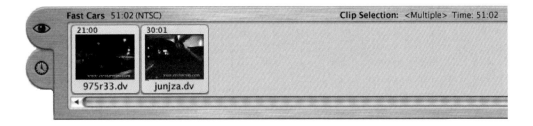

iMovie 2: **DON'T TOUCH THAT TOGGLE**

If you spend a lot of time switching between your digital camcorder and editing your clips, you'll love this tip: You can toggle back and forth without dragging that tiny blue button—instead try a larger target—just click on the filmstrip icon to edit, or the DV camera icon to import. This also works for the Volume Slider in the Monitor window. If you click on the left speaker icon, the slider moves all the way to the left (mute), and if you click on the right speaker icon, it jumps to full volume.

   iMovie 2: **ONE-CLICK IMPORTING**

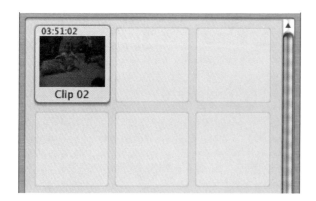

If you want to import the raw footage from your digital camcorder, rather than individual clips, connect your camera and just press the Spacebar. This not only starts your camera, but begins importing your footage immediately.

   iMovie 2: **YOU CAN ALWAYS GO HOME**

To quickly return to the beginning of your movie, you can click on the Home button (the button immediately to the left of the Play button) in the Monitor window; but you may find it quicker to just press the Home key on your keyboard.

   iMovie 2: **PRECISE NAVIGATION**

To Fast Forward one frame at a time, press Option-Right Arrow. To Rewind one frame at a time, press Option-Left Arrow. To move 10 frames at a time, just add the Shift key.

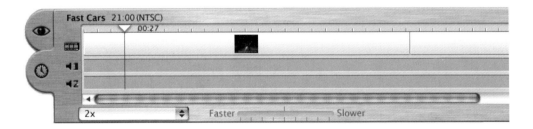

  iMovie 2: RAPID NAVIGATION

To quickly Fast Forward through your movie, instead of clicking the Fast Forward button shown below, press Command-] (right bracket). For a quick rewind press Command-[(left bracket). You don't have to hold the Bracket keys down, just press once to start the Playhead in motion, and press it once again to stop.

   iMovie 2: THE CLIP VIEWER'S VISUAL CUES

If you've adjusted the speed or direction of a clip, the Clip Viewer gives you a visual cue with tiny black icons just above the clip itself (in the upper-right corner of the clip's "slide mount"), to let you know just what you did. Two right-facing arrows show that you sped up the clip. A vertical line with one right-facing arrow lets you know the clip has been slowed down (for a slow-motion effect). A left-facing arrow tells you you've reversed the clip (it plays backward). If you've added a built-in iMovie effect (like Black & White, Sepia Tone, etc.) the letters "fx" appear. If you add a title to your clip, expect a "T" to appear.

   iMovie 2: UNDO, UNDO, UNDO, UNDO, UNDO, UNDO +4

If you realize you've made a mistake while in iMovie, as long as you catch your mistake fairly quickly (and before you empty the Trash), you may be in luck. That's because iMovie gives you 10 undos. Just press Command-Z again and again until you come to your mistake, or you reach the 10th undo (which ironically is usually just one step before your mistake).

   iMovie 2: GETTING BACK CROPPED-OUT SCENES

When you crop a clip in iMovie, the cropped portion is put in the Trash and you can't access those cropped away areas. That is unless you know this little secret—if you need to get back to the original clip you imported, perfectly intact, believe it or not you can, as long as you haven't emptied the Trash. Just click on the cropped clip in the Timeline

or Clip Viewer, then go under the Advanced menu and choose Restore Clip Media. A dialog box will appear telling you how much you'll get back, and asking you to OK the process. Click Restore, and the original clip is back, in its entirety. This even works on title screens created, and then cropped, right from within iMovie 2.

iMovie 2: **VISUAL TRANSITION CUES**

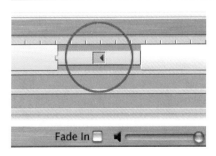

Once you drag a Transition into your Timeline or Clip Viewer, the icon of the Transition can sometimes give you a visual cue as to which Transition you dragged. Just look at the little arrows in the square window in the center of the Transition icon for a hint. To see the name of the Transition, click on it. If the default name doesn't help you (like the name "Push"), double-click on the Transition and enter a new name (like "1st clip slides 2nd clip over").

   iMovie 2: **GETTING MORE AUDIO TRACKS**

In the Timeline, there are three tracks where audio can go: The top timeline where the video clips are located also supports any audio from your digital camcorder's microphone that was captured when you shot your clips. The second track is usually used for sound effects or a narrator track. The third is usually used for background music. So you'd

think you'd be limited to three tracks, but actually, iMovie 2 lets you continue to import and lay multiple audio tracks right over one another. For example, if you have a music score on the bottom track and you import a sound effect, you'll notice that its little bar icon appears right on top of your score track's icon. It also plays right over it—not knocking it out—but playing right along with it. This enables you to use more than just the three tracks it appears you're limited to.

iMovie 2: **HOW TO CHANGE A TITLE ANYTIME**

One of the great things about creating your titles in iMovie 2 is that they're always editable. If at any time you want to change the content of your title, just click on the clip and then click on the Titles button. Your current text, font, etc. all appear in that pane. To edit them, just type in your new text, change your fonts, etc., and then press the Update button to update your current title.

   iMovie 2: **MUTING YOUR CAMERA'S AUDIO TRACK**

If you're putting a music track behind your movie and you don't want to hear the audio that was captured by your digital camcorder's built-in microphone, you can turn off the audio track for your camera clips. Just go to the Timeline Viewer, and at the far right of the viewer, uncheck the top checkbox.

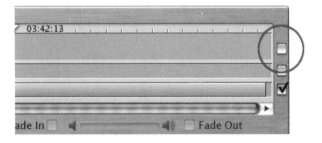

iMovie 2: **MORE CONTROL OVER AUDIO FADES**

The default settings for the Fade In/Out checkboxes at the bottom of the Timeline Viewer are, well...pretty darn lame (at best). The fades seem much too abrupt, and I've never been happy with their canned results. So, if you want to get more control over when your audio clips fade in/out, just double-click on your audio clip in the Timeline Viewer and a pane will come up where you can choose which fade you want, and control exactly how long your fade in/out takes using the two sliders. You'll never settle for that default fade again.

   iMovie 2: **CONTROLLING SOUND FX VOLUMES**

If you import sound effects (or use the built-in sound effects) you can control the volume of each sound effect individually. Just click directly on the sound effect you want to adjust (in the Timeline Viewer) then move the main volume slider to the level you'd like the effect to play. iMovie will keep track of each sound effect's individual volume and adjust them accordingly as your movie plays.

iMovie 2: **SEND IMPORTED CLIPS STRAIGHT TO THE TIMELINE**

By default, imported clips appear on the Shelf, and then once imported, you can drag them individually to the Timeline Viewer. However, if you'd like, you can change one preference setting and iMovie 2 will send your clips straight to the Timeline Viewer instead. You do this by going under the iMovie menu, under Preferences, and clicking on the Import tab. Under "Imported Clips Go To" choose Movie, and from now on, all imported clips will appear in the Timeline Viewer, rather than the shelf.

   iMovie 2: **MAKING STILL IMAGES STICK AROUND**

When you import a still image into iMovie 2 (from Photoshop, a scanned image, a screen capture, etc.), you can determine how long the still image will stay on screen.

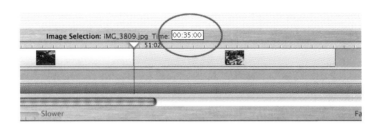

Just click on the image in the Timeline or Clip Viewer, and just above the clip (to the right of where the still clip's name appears), you'll see a field for Time. The still's current duration (usually 5 seconds—by default) will appear in that field, but you can highlight it and choose any amount of time that you'd like.

   iMovie 2: GIVING STILLS LESS SCREEN TIME

By default, when you import a still clip into iMovie 2, it stays on screen for 5 seconds. But if you'd like this default setting to be shorter (or longer) iMovie lets you change it to whatever you'd like. Just go under the iMovie menu, under Preferences, click on the Import tab, and at the bottom of the pane where it says "Still Clips are 5 seconds by default," highlight the number 5 and type in whatever length (in seconds) you'd like.

   iMovie 2: DON'T LET SOUND FX STOP YOU FROM INSERTING CLIPS

If you've meticulously added sound effects to your movie, and you've sync'd them to events in your clips, you might think twice about

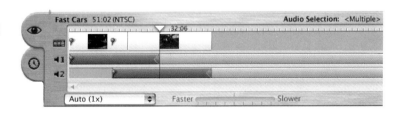

inserting a clip in your movie because it would slide down all the video clips that come after your insertion point to accommodate this new clip—making your movie longer—but leaving all your audio clips in their original spots. Now all your sound FX will be out of sync by the amount of time your imported clip takes. To get around this, before you import your click, Shift-click on each sound effect in your audio track, then press Command-L to "lock" your audio clips to your video clips. That way, when you insert your new clip, and all the video clips move over to accommodate the new track, all the sound fx clips will move right along with them.

iPhoto: **DUMP THE SHADOW**

You know that little drop shadow that appears behind your thumbnail images in the Photo Viewing Area? If it gets on your nerves, you can ditch it by pressing Command-Y to bring up iPhoto's Preferences. In the Preferences dialog, under Photos, click on the Frame button and the shadow effect is removed and is replaced by a thin white border around the thumbnail of your photo. While you're there, you can change the background color behind your thumbnails from white to any shade of gray or solid black, using the slider in the Frame section.

   iPhoto: **EDITING IPHOTO IMAGES IN PHOTOSHOP**

iPhoto lets you adjust a variety of aspects of your image, from tonal adjustments to removing red-eye, in iPhoto's built in image editor. However, if you prefer to edit your images in another application (such as Adobe Photoshop or Photoshop Elements), you can configure iPhoto to launch the editing application of your choice when you double-click on the image inside iPhoto. You do this by pressing Command-Y to bring up iPhoto's Preferences dialog. In the prefs dialog, where it says "Double-clicking photos opens them in" click on the "Other" button, navigate to the application you want to designate as your editing app, and then click OK. Now when you double-click a photo, your photo will open in your designated image-editing application.

   iPhoto: SKIP THE NEW ALBUM BUTTON

If you want to start a new album, skip the "New Album" button. You can save time by just selecting one (or more) images that you want in your new album, and then drag them over to the Album pane—a new album will be created for you automatically. A little red circle will appear in the bottom-right corner of the image you're dragging to let you know how many images you're dragging into this new album.

   iPhoto: CHANGING YOUR TUNE

When you choose to view your images using iPhoto's Slide Show option, iPhoto plays an acoustic guitar version of *Minuet in G*, which is great if you're viewing a slide show of baby photos, but isn't so great if you're viewing photos of David Lee Roth in concert. To change the background music that plays during the slide show, press Command-Y to bring up iPhoto's Preferences window. In the prefs window, under Slide Show, under Music, choose Other from the pop-up menu. Then, choose an MP3 file from your iTunes collection (by the way, it must be an MP3 file). Close the Preferences window, and when you run the slide show again, it will now feature your MP3 selection as the background music.

iPhoto: GETTING PHOTOS FROM YOUR DRIVE INTO IPHOTO

If you're new to iPhoto, and you want to import photos from your hard drive, the natural thing to do is click on the Import button at the bottom of the Photo Viewing area, right? The Import Toolbar appears, but unless you have a digital camera connected to your Mac, the Import button will be grayed out. To get those images from your hard drive right into iPhoto, skip the Import button and instead go under the File menu and choose Import. A standard Open dialog will appear so you can navigate to the folder of images you want to import.

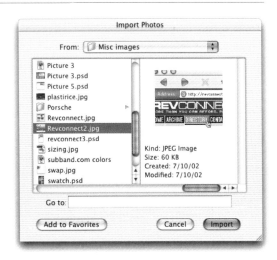

   iPhoto: WHEN IPHOTO DELETES, WHEN IT DOESN'T

If you delete a photo from an album, that doesn't actually delete the photo from your hard drive—it just removes the photo from that particular album—the original photo still resides within your Photo Library. But be careful: when you delete an image from the Photo Library, you're deleting it from your drive (for good).

iPhoto: **WHAT TO DO WHEN ALL GOES WRONG**

If you've edited, cropped, and otherwise adjusted an image in iPhoto, and after looking at the results, you wish you really hadn't, you can actually start over—from scratch—and get back your clean un-retouched original image. You do this by selecting the image, going under the File menu, and choosing "Revert to Original." Okay, but what if you set up iPhoto to let you edit your image in another application, such as Photoshop? Believe it or not—Revert to Original still works.

   iPhoto: **ROTATING IN THE OPPOSITE DIRECTION**

When you press the Rotate image button, by default it rotates your image counterclockwise. If you want to rotate your image clockwise, just hold the Option key before you click the rotate button.

iPhoto: DEALING WITH LONG COMMENTS

iPhoto lets you add comments to your photos, and you can use these comments to help you sort, categorize, or just make notes about a particular photo. These comments are entered in the Comments field, which appears in a field below the Info panel (if you don't see the Info panel, click on the button with the little "i" on it on the bottom-left side). If you add a long comment for a particular photo, iPhoto will accommodate you, but you won't be able to scroll down and see your entire comment because the Comments field doesn't have scroll bars. There's only one way to see your entire comment—and that's to click on the little circle at the top of the Info panel and drag upward to make more of your comment visible.

iPhoto: RENAMING ALBUMS

If you click on an Album, even though its title appears in the Info panel, it's grayed out and you can't edit its name there—instead, just double-click on the album in the Album panel, and its name will highlight, ready for you to type in a new name.

iPhoto: **CHANGING FONTS IN BOOK MODE**

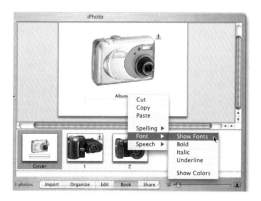

If you're creating a book in Book mode, you can edit the font used in any page by highlighting the text and then Control-clicking on it. A pop-up menu will appear where you can choose the font, size, type style, and type color of your choice.

   iPhoto: **CUSTOMIZING THE EDIT TOOLBAR**

If you want more control over editing your images in iPhoto, press Command-Y to bring up the Preferences window, and where it says "Double-clicking photos opens them in" choose "Separate Window." Then, when you double-click a photo to edit it, your image opens into a different environment, giving

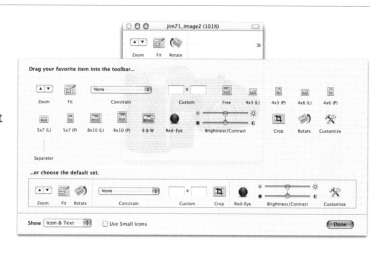

you more control over your editing process, including the ability to customize the Toolbar that appears at the top of the window. Just Control-click on the Toolbar, and a pop-up menu will appear where you can choose "Customize Toolbar." This brings up a large sheet full of different tools for different tasks, and it works very much like customizing the Toolbar in Finder windows—just drag the icons you want in your Toolbar up to it. To reorder the tools, just drag their icons, and to remove a tool, just drag it off the bar.

iPhoto: **EDIT IN PHOTOSHOP WITHOUT SETTING PREFS**

Earlier, we showed how to set up iPhoto to let you edit your photos in a separate image-editing application

(such as Photoshop) by changing your iPhoto Preferences. But here's a great tip if you only occasionally want to edit your photos in a separate application—just drag the thumbnail of your photo right from the Photo Viewing area, onto the Photoshop icon right in the Dock, and your image will be opened in Photoshop (or of course, you can drag it to any other image-editing program just as easily, but really, why would you?).

   iPhoto: **SUPERSIZE THAT PHOTO**

If you want to quickly see a photo from your Photo Viewing area at a very large size, just click on the Share button, and then

in the Toolbar at the bottom, click on the Desktop button. Your selected image will be set as your desktop image and will take over the entire screen (and it's huge!).

   iPhoto: **PUTTING YOUR COVER SHOT INSIDE THE BOOK**

There will be times where you
want the photo you chose for
the cover to be also included
inside your book (perhaps
because you want to add a
different caption, or you want
to pair it with another photo
inside, or maybe you want to

show it without a caption at all). To do this, all you have to do is duplicate the photo.
You do this by clicking on the photo you want to duplicate and pressing Command-D.

   iPhoto: **CREATING YOUR OWN EDITING WINDOW**

If you've got a lot of editing to do on an image in
iPhoto, you'll probably find it helpful to open
that image in its own separate editing window
(with its own separate customized Toolbar). To
do that, in the Organize section, click on the
photo you want to edit, then press the Edit
button. When in Edit mode, hold the Option key
and double-click on the photo and it will appear
in a separate editing window.

Preview: CONVERTING TO TIFF, JPEG, OR PHOTOSHOP

Want to change most any graphic into a
Photoshop file? Just open the file in Preview,
go under the File menu, and choose Export,
where you can export your graphic in
Photoshop format. But you're not limited to
Photoshop format—Preview will also export
your file as a JPEG, PICT, QuickTime (to open
in QuickTime Player), BMP (for sharing files
with PC users), PICT, Targa (for video) and
more. If the format you're saving in has
options (such as quality and compression
settings for JPEG and TIFF images), click the
Options button in the Export dialog box to
access those controls.

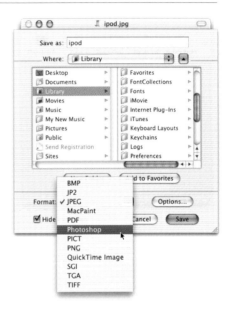

Preview: ROTATING IMAGES WITHOUT THE TOOLBAR

If you prefer to work in Preview
with the Toolbar hidden (you hide
it by pressing the white pill-shaped
button at the top-right corner of
Preview's title bar), you can still
access probably the most important
command from the Toolbar:
rotation—especially important if
you're viewing images from your
digital camera in Preview. Just
press Command-L to rotate your
image to the left, or Command-R
to rotate your image to the right.

Preview: CUSTOMIZE PREVIEW'S TOOLBAR

Like the Finder itself,
Preview's Toolbar is very
customizable and you can
easily adjust it so that only
the tools that you want will
appear in the Toolbar in the
order that you want them.
You do this by Control-clicking
anywhere in Preview's
Toolbar, and a pop-up menu
will appear where you can
choose Customize Toolbar. A
Sheet will slide down with
various tool icons that you can
drag right up to the Toolbar. If there's a tool you don't want in the Toolbar, while this
Sheet is still open, just click-and-drag them off.

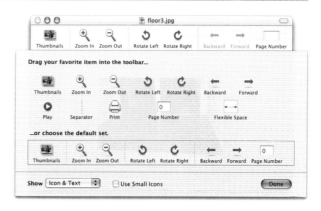

Preview: TOOLBAR ICONS TAKING UP TOO MUCH ROOM?

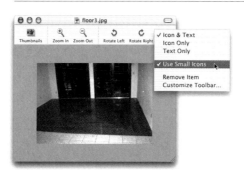

If Preview's Toolbar icons and text are
taking up too much room (some of your
tools aren't visible, etc.), just Control-click
anywhere in the Toolbar and choose "Use
Small Icons," and the current icons will be
replaced with significantly smaller versions
that take up much less room.

Preview: **TOGGLE THRU TOOLBAR VIEWS**

Command-click on the pill-shaped button in the upper-right corner of Preview's title bar, and each time you click you'll get another view that's smaller than the default Toolbar view (which is large icons and large text). Click once, you'll get smaller icons. Click again—icons with no text, smaller icons with no text, then just text, and then really small text. Of course, if you don't want the Toolbar visible at all, simply click once on the pill-shaped button, and it will hide itself out of view.

Preview: **SWITCHING THUMBNAIL SIDES (GO LEFT, NOT RIGHT)**

If you open a PDF file in Preview, you can see thumbnails of the pages in your PDF document by pressing Command-T. A little pane pops out to the right side of Preview's window displaying tiny thumbnail images of each page. These are clickable and enable you to jump right to the page you want. However, if you'd prefer that this pop-out pane appear on the left side of your screen, rather than the right, simply drag your Preview window to the right side of your screen before you press Command-T. Now, it will pop out to the left.

   Preview: **SAVING GRAPHICS AS PDFs**

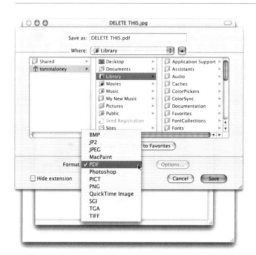

While in Preview, you can save any open graphic file as a PDF by going under the File menu and choosing Export. When the Export dialog appears, choose PDF from the Format pop-up menu (it's the default, so unless you've been saving in another format, it should already be there). Click Save, and Preview will create a PDF for you.

   Preview: **PRINTING FINDER WINDOWS**

Since Mac OS X doesn't have the ability to print Finder windows (like in previous versions of the OS), here's a popular workaround: Make a screen capture of the window (Shift-Command-4 and drag a marquee around the window) which saves the capture as a PDF file on your desktop. Double-click on your

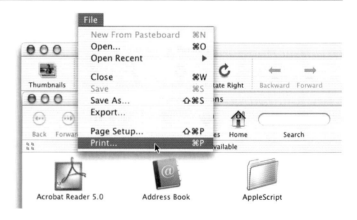

PDF screen capture to open it in Preview, and then you can print the image from within Preview, producing a printed view of your Finder window (just like in "the old days").

DVD Player: **TAKING CONTROL**

It seems that it would make sense that
Apple's DVD player would share the
same keyboard shortcuts as the
QuickTime Player, since they're both
motion-graphics players, and they're
both from Apple. Ah, if life were only
that simple. While the Up/Down Arrow
keys work for controlling the volume in
the QuickTime player, you have to press Command-Up/Down Arrow to control volume in
the DVD player (the same volume shortcuts as iTunes). But while you mute iTunes by
pressing Option-Command-Down Arrow, you press Command-K to mute the DVD player.
Thankfully, one important command is the same no matter which player you're using—
pressing the Spacebar starts or pauses movies in the DVD player.

   DVD Player: **MOVIES ON THE BIG SCREEN**

DVDs were made for the big
screen, so don't put yourself
through the trauma of watching
your DVD movies in the player—
instead press Command-0 to make
your movie go "full screen." After
it's up and running, press Control-
C to hide the controller, and then
you can work the DVD player using
the keyboard shortcuts given in the
previous tip.

CHAPTER 12 • Digital Hub Apps   **239**

DVD Player: **AUTO-CONTROLLER HIDING**

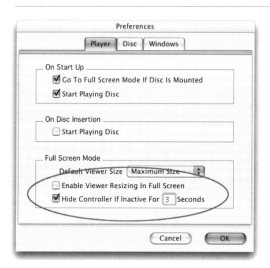

Once you've started a DVD in Full Screen mode, by default the Controller will automatically hide itself after a 10-second period of inactivity. If this isn't long enough for you, or if 10 seconds seems too long (you just want to hit play and have it go away almost immediately) you can change the duration by going under the DVD menu, under Preferences, and in the Player tab enter a new time (in seconds) for the field named "Hide Controller if Inactive For __ Seconds."

 DVD Player: **GET ME BACK TO THE MAIN MENU**

One of the most important keyboard shortcuts to me is the ability to get back to the main DVD menu while the DVD is already playing. To get there, just press Command-~ (the key just above the Tab key) and it will cycle you back to the DVD's Main Menu.

DVD Player: **CONTROLLER MAXIMUS**

If you're wondering whether the DVD player is missing some DVD functionality, you're half right. It does have the ability to access DVD controls, such as slow motion, subtitling, camera angles, language, etc., but for the sake of space considerations, they're tucked away. To bring these buttons into view, click on the three little dots on the right center of the Player and the Player will expand to show two additional rows of buttons.

   DVD Player: **GOING VERTICAL**

Tired of the boring horizontal player? Maybe it's time to get vertical. Just press Shift-Command-V and a vertical version of the player appears.

   iDVD: **WHAT TO DO WHEN IT WON'T ACCEPT IMOVIE CLIPS**

Unfortunately, when you capture video through iMovie, you can't just draw the raw source file right into iDVD 2. That's because iMovie uses the DVStream codec, while iDVD 2 uses the regular DV Codec. Luckily, this is pretty easy to fix. Just go to the File menu and choose Export Movie. In the dialog that appears, under Export, choose For iDVD. This creates a regular DV codec file where the audio and video appear on separate tracks (whereas in DVStream format, both the audio and video are in the same track). Now you can drag this newly exported file right into iDVD 2 without a problem.

   iDVD: **WHICH SETTINGS WORK BEST FOR IMPORTING**

iDVD 2 supports most of the same video and image file formats that QuickTime does, so if your video-editing app can export to QuickTime, you can probably use these movies in your iDVD project. To get the best results, here are some QuickTime export settings you can try: Choose DV-NTSC with a frame rate of 29.97 (if you're creating video that will be viewed outside the US, use PAL-DV with a frame rate of 25). For audio, choose No Compression and set the rate to 48 KHz. Also, for best quality on screen, don't use QuickTime movies that are smaller than the DVD standard size of 720x480 pixels.

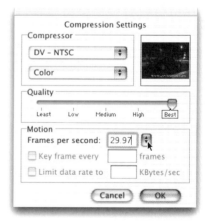

iDVD: **GETTING RID OF THE APPLE LOGO WATERMARK**

I'm never one to deny Apple its props, and I love the Apple logo (in fact I have an Apple logo sticker on my car and at least one-third of my clothing), but the one place I don't want it to appear is on my iDVD projects (where it appears by default as a watermark). If you're like me, and want it to go away, just go under the iDVD menu, under Preferences, and turn off the "Show Watermark" checkbox.

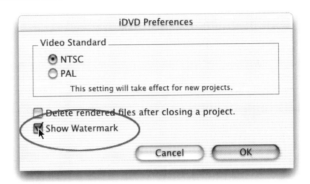

   iDVD: **MOVING YOUR IDVD 2 PROJECT TO ANOTHER MAC**

If you're thinking of moving your iDVD project from your Mac to another Mac, make sure you move all of the source files (both still images and movies) you used in your project right along with it. You'll need to, because iDVD references those files, and without them, you're pretty much out of luck. Your best bet is probably to store all your source files in the same folder as your iDVD project file,

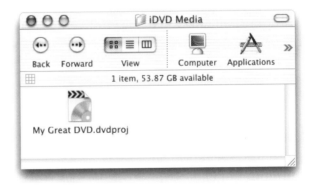

that way (a) you won't forget them when copying, and (b) you don't have to worry about iDVD going to search for them—they're right there.

   iDVD: BEATING THE SLIDE SHOW LIMIT

While it's true that iDVD limits your slide show to just 99 slides, iDVD does allow you to have multiple slide shows on the same disc, so your only real limitation is that can only show 99 at a time.

   iDVD: THE MISSING MOTION MENUS FROM BURNED DVDS

If you burn a DVD and you don't get the motion menus or motion backgrounds, here's an easy fix: Before you burn your DVD, make sure you have the Motion button checked (turned on), or the motion menus, buttons, and audio won't be available when you try to play your disc.

iDVD: **GETTING BETTER RESULTS FROM IMOVIE EXPORTS**

Have you ever exported an iMovie clip to iDVD, but when you view the clips they're pretty ratty looking? If you're thinking of spending the thousand bucks for Final Cut Pro to get better results—you don't have to. What you need is to download the free iMovie upgrade to at least version 2.0.3 which has been optimized for dramatically better iMovie export to iDVD format. Once you've downloaded and installed the upgrade, try re-exporting your iMovie clips—you'll be amazed at the difference.

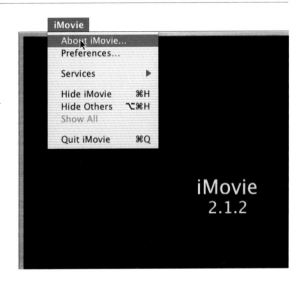

   iDVD: **SETTING THE TRACK ORDER**

This one throws a lot of people, because moving the clips around in the iDVD menu doesn't actually change the Track List Order on the DVD. To put the clips in the order that you want them to appear on the DVD (so you can bypass the menu altogether and just shuttle from one track to the next), drag each clip (one at a time) to the iDVD window. Double-check the order by clicking Theme to open the Themes drawer and then click Status.

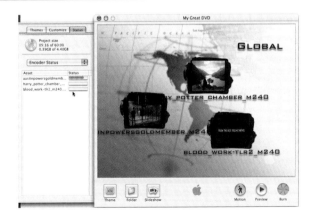

I smell trouble

TROUBLE-SHOOTING TIPS

If Mac OS X is the most stable operating system in the world, why do we need a troubleshooting chapter? Well, this chapter really isn't about

I SmellT-r-o-u-b-l-e

troubleshooting tips

system crashes—it's more about dealing with applications that freeze up and stuff like that. In fact, Mac OS X is so amazingly stable I'm not sure you could write an entire chapter on system crashes. In fact, I know many Mac OS X users that have never had even one system crash—it works all day, every day, flawlessly. Outside of Mac OS X users, you'd be hard-pressed to find anyone else on this entire planet who's never experienced Microsoft Windows' "blue screen of death." Okay, admittedly, I did once hear about a man in Walpole, Massachusetts (a retired CPA), who only uses his PC for writing letters to his brother in Novi, Michigan (a retired airline pilot). They don't get along all that well, so he only writes him two or three times a year, and then mostly to complain about a pustulated bunion on his left foot that's the size of a Titleist Pro V1. Thus far, his PC hasn't crashed. But it's comin'. Oh yes, bunion man—it's a-comin'.

   SOMETHING'S WRONG: TRY THIS FIRST

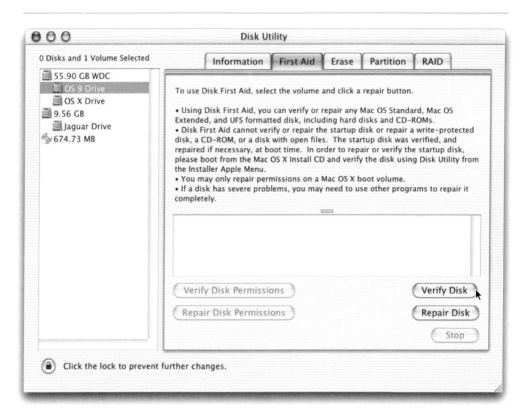

If your Mac starts acting funky, it's time to reach for Disk First Aid. In Mac OS X, Disk First Aid is part of Disk Utility—a free utility program that comes with Mac OS X, and it's the first place I go when things get hairy. Because Disk First Aid won't (can't, refuses to) repair your startup disk, you'll have to start up from your Mac OS X install disk (just restart, and hold the letter "C" while the system is booting to start up from your install disk, rather than the system on your hard drive). Once restarted from your CD, click on the Installer, then choose Open Disk Utility. Once Disk Utility opens, click on the First Aid tab, then click on the drive you want to repair and click the Repair button.

MAC MESSED UP? TRY THIS NEXT

If Disk First Aid doesn't fix your Mac's "wonkyness," you should probably try the age-old Mac repair trick known as "Zapping the PRAM." (This resets the battery-powered memory that retains all your Mac preferences after you've shut down your Mac. Zapping it resets everything back to the factory default settings.) Restart your Mac and hold Option-Command-P-R (that's the letter "P" and the letter "R"—hold them both down, along with Option-Command). Keep holding these down and your Mac will "bong" and restart over and over again. Let it go through this "bonging and restarting thing" at least three times, then release the keys you've been holding down, and let your Mac go through its regular startup routine. This can fix a number of your Mac's ills. (Note: Don't be surprised if one the preferences it resets is your startup disk back to OS 9.)

  IN AN EMERGENCY, THEY BREAK THE GLASS

I said on the back cover and in the introduction that I wasn't going to include any UNIX, and in keeping with that promise, I'm not going to even open the Terminal Window (your Mac's evil gateway into its UNIX soul, where really scary command line stuff takes place). However, I'm going to just mention, in passing, about a great Mac OS X repair technique used by some UNIX-using people. Now, because I'm simply relating a story about how other people use a UNIX-y repair trick, instead of telling you how to do it, I'm not really teaching you UNIX. Hey, if you wind up learning something by my simply relating their story, that's not my fault, right?

Well, here's what those UNIX hooligans do—they restart their Macs, but on restart they hold the Command key and the "s" key. Shortly, a list of scary-looking commands appears on their screen, then they type "fsck-y" (note: after the "k", type a space, the minus sign, and then the letter "y.") then press the Return key. This invokes some sort of freaky UNIX ritual in which line after line of UNIX mumbo-jumbo starts scrolling up their screen in white reversed text on a black background. If their Mac is OK, it'll say so—"The volume appears to be OK." If that's the case, they just type "reboot" and go on with their lives. However, If there's a problem found on their machine, it reads "File System Modified," which means "uh-oh." If they get the "File System Modified" message, it seems that they repeat the process of typing in "fsck-y" and then hitting the Return key, again and again, until "The volume appears to be OK" finally appears (which they say, usually takes just a few tries). Then they too can type "reboot" and their Macs restart as usual. These people reportedly then go on to live otherwise productive lives knowing that they cheated death, used UNIX, and lived to fight another day.

DEALING WITH PROBLEMS IN CLASSIC MODE

If you run into problems while in Classic mode, you can use many of the old pre-OS X trouble-shooting tips (disabling the Extensions from loading, bringing up the Extensions Manager on startup, rebuilding the desktop, etc.). The great thing is, you don't have to remember all those keyboard shortcuts, because Mac OS X will let you choose which Classic startup tweaks you want to do in Classic, while you're still in

Mac OS X. Just go to the System Preferences and click on the Classic icon. In the Classic pane, click on the Advanced tab. You'll see a pop-up menu where you can choose to have Classic open the Extension manager, and even a button for rebuilding the desktop—not to mention a button for restarting Classic altogether.

HOW TO DEAL WITH EL CRASHO GRANDE

If Mac OS X has such a momentous crash that it disables your whole machine (this has only happened to me twice), all you can really do is shut down and restart. If you're sure you've really crashed and all hope is lost, you can usually restart by pressing Shift-Option-Command and the Power On Button (if your keyboard has one—Apple's latest keyboard sadly doesn't have one and that tweaks me to no end). If you don't have a Power On key on the keyboard, press-and-hold the one on your Mac itself and after a few seconds, it should shut down, and then you can restart by simply pushing the Power On key again.

WHEN FILES DON'T WANT TO BE TRASHED

If you have a file that clearly has a burning will to live on, because it won't let you drag it into the Trash, here are a couple of things to help you shorten its life span:

(1) Click on the stubborn file, press Command-I to open its Info window, and check to see if the "Locked" checkbox is turned on. If it is, turn it off and then it should accept its new life in the ol' dump-a-roo.

(2) If the reluctant document is in a folder (or if it's a folder itself), click on the folder, then press Command-I to open its Info window. Click on the right-facing gray triangle to the left of the words "Ownership & Permissions" to reveal that pane. Assuming you're the Administrator (or assuming that this is your Mac and you're the only one that uses it), in the pop-up menu for "Owner," change from Read Only to Read & Write. Now, you should be able to move your document/folder into the Trash.

   UN-FORGETTING YOUR PASSWORD

What do you do if you forget your administrator password? Believe it or not, you're not SOL (suddenly out of luck. Okay, we both know that word isn't suddenly, but for the sake of my editors, let's pretend it is). To get around your forgotten password, you'll need your original Mac OS X installer disc. Put it in your CD-ROM drive, restart your Mac, and as soon it begins to restart hold down the letter "C" on your keyboard (this tells your Mac to boot from the CD, rather than the system on your drive). Double-click on the Installer, and then choose Reset Password. When the dialog appears, choose which disk you want to access, then type in a new user name and password, then click the Save button, and quit the Reset Password dialog, then quit the Installer program. That's it. When you restart your Mac, you can use your new User Name and Password. I know what you're thinking—shouldn't this have been in the Mac OS Pranks chapter? Probably, but I just didn't have the heart.

WHEN YOUR APPLICATION FREEZES UP

It happens: You're working along, not doing anything earth-shattering (you're not splitting atoms, reanalyzing the national debt, etc.), and your current application just freezes. The good news is—this freeze affects only your current application—all other running applications and the system itself are just fine. The bad news—you'll have to force quit, so any unsaved documents are, well, unsaved. To force quit, press Option-Command-Esc to bring up the Force Quit dialog (or Option-Control-click on the frozen application's icon in the dock and choose Force Quit from the pop-up).

 CHICKENING OUT OF A FORCE QUIT

When you go to force quit an application, the Force Quit window appears, where you can choose which application you want to force quit. If this window is open and you decide force quitting is not what you wanted to do (in other words, you "chicken out"), instead of clicking the Force Quit button (which force quits the high-lighted application) just press Command-W to close the window, and you've effectively "chickened out."

TURN ON THE CRASH EARLY-WARNING SYSTEM

This tip is bordering on geek-dom, so before you use it, it wouldn't hurt to grab the nearest pocket protector before you read any further. If you crash, you can ask Mac OS X to let you know why you crashed (but you have to turn this feature on before the crash—it's turned off by default). Perhaps more important than that, if this feature is turned on, it may pop up and warn you that something's wrong, just before you crash—giving you just enough time to save your open documents. To turn this "crash early-warning system" on, look inside your hard drive, inside your Utilities folder, and launch an application called "Console." From the Console menu, choose "Preferences," and in the Preferences panel click on the Crashes tab. Then, click on the checkboxes for "Enable crash reporting" and "Automatically display crash logs." If you crash (or in some cases if you're about to crash), a window will appear with a log of what's happened, or what's about to happen. That's your cue.

 THE SILENT SUBWOOFER

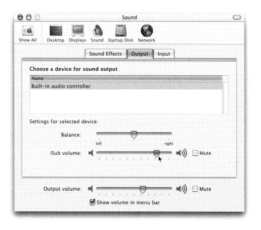

This is just a quick tip to keep iSub owners from pulling their hair out (the iSub is a way-cool, clear plastic audio subwoofer from Harman/Kardon made specifically for use with iMacs). When you first install Jaguar, you may notice that your iSub isn't working. That's because in Jaguar the iSub has its own separate volume setting, and by default it's completely turned off. To turn it back on (and start kickin' some nasty bass) go under the Apple menu, under System Preferences, and click on the Sound icon, and then click on the Output tab. If you have an iSub connected to your iMac, you'll see an "iSub Volume" slider, and it will be set to its lowest possible setting (off). Drag the slider to the right to start pumpin' the bass until the glass in your office starts to rattle. Remember: If it's too loud—you're too old.

   ## WHEN ALL ELSE FAILS, REINSTALL

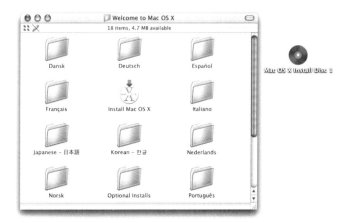

If you've tried just about everything and your Mac is still acting up, there comes a point when you realize that you're going to have to do a full reinstall. This isn't a bad thing—you're not reinstalling Windows. And luckily, this doesn't reformat your drive—it doesn't erase or uninstall your applications—in fact, it doesn't mess with your Home folder at all—it just reinstalls your System stuff (that's the technical term: "System stuff"). To do a reinstall, insert your Mac OS CD, restart holding down the "C" key (to start up off the CD), and then run the installer. It sounds like a lot of trouble, but it's really not, and doing a reinstall will usually fix all that ails your Mac. It's like the "Magic Fix-it Potion," and now that it's so easy, you don't have to fear a reinstall any more.

   ## PANIC ROOM

Now don't panic, but there's a chance that one day you will—panic, that is. That's right—a full fledged "running down the halls screaming" total freak-out type of panic. This will occur should you, or a loved one, encounter the dreaded "Kernel Panic." (This is the same term used to describe a situation that happened back in the 1970s at local KFCs if they thought the restaurant's namesake was going to drop by unannounced [okay, that was bad. Sorry]). Actually, a Kernel Panic appears without warning, right in the middle of your work, as a black screen packed with frightening UNIX code. The fix? Just restart right away, and chances are the panic will immediately subside (the Mac's—not yours). It will probably never rear its ugly head again. If for some reason, restarting doesn't do the trick (get this), just restart again. Okay, does it seem like simply restarting one's Mac cures just about everything? Yup—it sure seems like that.

TRASHIN' THE PREFS

If you have an application that keeps crashing for some unexplained reason, it may be because its preferences file has become corrupt. This is more common than you might think, and luckily fixing it is easier than you might think. Just go to your Home folder, inside your Library folder, inside your Preferences folder, locate the preferences file for the application, and drag it into the Trash (the file might be in a folder with the application's name). Restarting your application will

rebuild a new factory-fresh set of preferences, and this will often take care of your problem. A good hint that a corrupt preferences file is the root of the problem is if somethings looks wrong within the application itself. For example, in Photoshop I've seen tools missing, menu commands suddenly missing, and handles missing from bounding boxes. Trashing Photoshop's preferences file fixed all these problems in just seconds.

   WHEN "TRASHIN THE PREFS" DOESN'T WORK

If deleting the preferences file doesn't fix your application's problems, it might be time for (you guessed it) a reinstall of your application. Before you do, make sure you trash the preferences file (as detailed in the previous tip) and delete the application itself by dragging it into the Trash. Then put your application install disc in the CD-ROM drive, and get to it.

   FROZEN IN THE DOCK

This particular problem (freezing a Dock icon in its magnified view, or the whole Dock itself just freezes up) usually happens to me when I'm toggling back and forth between an application running in Classic mode and one running in Mac OS X. Luckily, fixing the problem usually just requires force quitting the Dock itself. You do this by going to your Applications folder, inside the Utilities folder, and double-click on a utility called Process Viewer. Once launched,

Name	User	Status	% CPU	% Memory
mDNSResponder	root	Running	0.00	0.10
loginwindow	tommaloney	Running	0.20	0.70
cupsd	root	Running	0.00	0.10
configd	root	Running	0.00	0.20
crashreporterd	root	Running	0.00	0.00
ATSServer	tommaloney	Running	11.60	0.30
autodiskmount	root	Running	0.00	0.00
Window Manager	tommaloney	Running	26.90	3.70
Process Viewer	tommaloney	Running	30.80	0.50
kextd	root	Running	0.00	0.10
coreservicesd	root	Running	0.20	2.10
DirectoryService	root	Running	0.00	0.30
pbs	tommaloney	Running	0.00	0.10
Dock	tommaloney	Running	0.00	1.00

Find: _____ Show: All Processes

Process Listing

42 processes   Sample every 20 seconds

▶ More Info

you'll see the Dock listed in the Process Listing. To force quit it, just double-click on the word "Dock."

   AVOID THE CRASHING BLUES

If you want to bring on problems—bad stuff like Kernel Panics, crashes, freezes, bronchitis, etc.—a sure way to bring those about is to delete or rename files or folders that Mac OS X needs to do its thing. Some of these are invisible files (I know, if I can't see them, how I can delete them? They become visible when you're accessing your machine across a network, or if you boot from Mac OS 9), and some are files and folders on the root directory. If you rename them, that freaks the OS out. The real danger for this happening is when you have booted in Mac OS 9, because when you do, the OS no longer protects these files and folders (they're locked and protected in Mac OS X). So basically, if you've booted in Mac OS 9, don't go messin' with stuff that looks strange to you (in other words, hands off anything you're not absolutely sure about— don't change its name, don't move it, and for sure don't delete it).

WHEN THE MAC WON'T LET YOU INSTALL A PROGRAM

This happens sometimes, even if you're the administrator. You double-click on an installer to install an application, and a large dialog box appears telling you "You need an Administrator's Password to install the software," but then it doesn't ask you for a password. What's the deal? All you have to do is click on the little lock icon at the bottom-left side of the dialog, where it says "Click the lock to make changes" and the password dialog appears (I know, it doesn't make much sense but that's the way it works). Once it appears, just enter your admin password, and then you can install the program. That is if you're the administrator (if you're a single user, and not sharing your machine with other users, or across a network, you're automatically the administrator).

   WHEN IT COMES TO TROUBLESHOOTING, YOU'RE NOT ALONE

One of the most amazing and gratifying things about Mac OS X is that it's so stable that there's just not that much troubleshooting stuff necessary. But needless to say, there's more to troubleshooting a computer than I can fit into this chapter, but you're not out of luck. That's because Apple has created a huge database of Macintosh problems and their solutions (called the Apple Knowledge Base) that you can access via their Web site at http://kbase.info.apple.com.

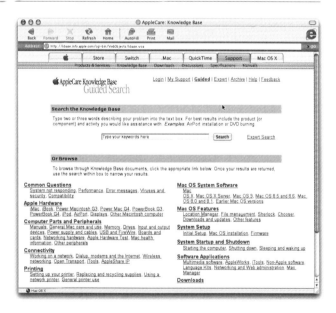

Hang on.
Help is on the way.

You may find this hard to believe, but this book is not the complete definitive resource for learning all the nuances, nooks, and crannies of an operating system as advanced as Mac OS X. (I know, shocking isn't it?) That's why I've included this Appendix—to lead you to my personal favorite resources (both books and Web sites) for learning more about Mac OS X (if that's possible).

   Must-have book: DR. MAC: THE OS X FILES

By Bob LeVitus
Wiley Publishing, Inc.
ISBN: 0-7645-1680-9
$34.99

I've been a fan of Bob's writing for years, and he really makes learning Mac OS X fun. There's a lot of great stuff in the book, including some very good troubleshooting info, and his personality comes through even when he's telling you how to deal with a flashing question mark. This is a more advanced book, so if you're starting to get good at Mac OS X, it's time to give this one a look.

   Must-have book: MAC OS X: THE MISSING MANUAL

By David Pogue
Published by O'Reilly/Pogue Press
ISBN 0-596-00082-0
$24.95

In my opinion, this is the absolute best book out there for really understanding Mac OS X from top to bottom, and as I mentioned in my acknowledgments, it's the book that got me really excited about Mac OS X. David Pogue's writing style, humor, and in-depth understanding of the subject make it a really fun and exciting way to learn. I can't recommend this book enough.

Must-have book: MACWORLD MAC OS X BIBLE

By Lon Poole and Dennis R. Cohen
Published by Hungry Minds
ISBN: 0-7645-3467-X
$34.99

I've always enjoyed Hungry Minds' "Bible" series for their completeness, and they make such a great resource because at nearly 900 pages, about everything you'd want to know about Mac OS X is in here. Also, at about 900 pages, you're probably not going to sit there and read it cover to cover like you would David Pogue's *Missing Manual*, but this is one you'll definitely want to keep on your bookshelf for the next time you "hit the wall" and need an answer fast.

Must-have book: MAC OS X UNLEASHED

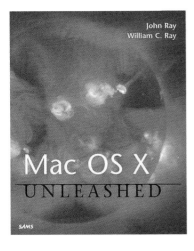

by John Ray, William C. Ray
Published by Sams
ISBN: 0-672-32229-3
$49.99

At 1,500 pages, this book can be used as a weapon for self-defense situations. Like the *Mac OS X Bible*, this is more of a reference work, but it's very complete and I can't think of anything that's not already in there. It's easy to read, fun, and the authors have really done a nice job of making some very technical aspects of Mac OS X very accessible. This is another one I'd recommend keeping on a handy bookshelf.

   ## Must-visit site: MACMINUTE

www.macminute.com

This is a really great Mac news site, and they're right on top of all the latest Mac OS X product announcements, updates, and news (they put a little aqua "X" in front of all Mac OS X news bites, so those stories really jump out at you). I particularly like their coverage of Apple corporate news, plus they keep a running list of key software releases in the sidebar of their home page, so even if you haven't been there in a few weeks, it takes just a quick glance to see if any of the apps you use have been updated or new versions released. Also, their "Executive Briefings" (a recap of the week's news) are outstanding. Although MacMinute, like Apple itself, leans toward Mac OS X users, Mac OS 9 users will love this concise, to-the-point, and cleanly designed site.

   ## Must-visit site: MAC OS X FAQ

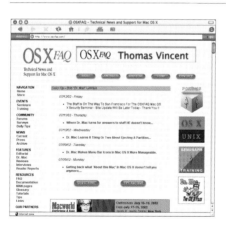

www.osxfaq.com

There's lots of news, tips, hints, and other current resources for helping you get ahead using Mac OS X. This is another great site, with loads of info, news, and a reader forum. Perhaps best of all is the fact that Bob LeVitus is all over the site, with a "Daily Tip" column, and a reprint of his Mac column from the *Houston Chronicle*.

Mac OS X
KillerTips

   Must-visit site: **MAC OS X HINTS**

www.macosxhints.com

This site rocks! It's got loads of tips, supplied by the site's own visitors, and it's a real thriving community of Mac OS X users helping others users and I can't say enough about it. Its editorial staff is first rate, and are actively involved in all the forums, with their own helpful suggestions and hints. The site is well designed, easy to use, and it's easy to find the things you're looking for. On a scale of 1-to-10, it's a 10!

   Must-visit site: **VERSION TRACKER**

www.versiontracker.com/macosx/index.shtml

This will probably wind up being one of your most-visited sites, because it's the central resource for getting the latest updates of Mac OS X applications, and for finding out which applications have been updated to Mac OS X. The site, which is hugely popular within the Mac community at large, especially with professional Macintosh consultants who make their living keeping their clients' machines running at peak performance with the least amount of problems, is fast-loading, well-designed, and it just flat-out works! Use it once, and you'll find it indispensable.

INDEX

COLOPHON

The book was produced by the authors and their design team using all Macintosh computers, including a Power Mac G4 450-MHz, a Power Mac G4 500-MHz, a Power Mac G4 Dual Processor 500-MHz, a Power Mac G4 733-MHz, a Power Mac G4 933-MHz, and an iMac. We use LaCie, Sony, and Apple Studio Display monitors.

Page layout was done using Adobe PageMaker 6.5 and Adobe InDesign 2.0. Scanning was done primarily on a UMAX PowerLook 1100 FireWire scanner. Our graphics server is a Power Mac G3, with a 60-GB LaCie external drive, and we burn our CDs to a TDK veloCD 32X CD-RW.

The headers for each technique are set in Adobe MyriadMM_565 SB 600 NO at 11 on 12.5 leading, with the Horizontal Scaling set to 100%. Body copy is set using Trebuchet at 9.5 points on 11.5 leading, with the Horizontal Scaling set to 100%.

Screen captures were made with Snapz Pro X and were placed and sized within Adobe PageMaker 6.5. The book was output at 150 line screen, and all in-house printing was done using a Tektronix Phaser 7700 by Xerox.

ADDITIONAL RESOURCES

ScottKelbyBooks.com
For information on Scott's other Macintosh and graphics-related books, visit his book site. For background info on Scott, visit www.scottkelby.com.

http://www.scottkelbybooks.com

Mac Design Magazine
Scott is Editor-in-Chief of *Mac Design Magazine*, "The Graphics Magazine for Macintosh Users." It's a tutorial-based print magazine with how-to columns on Photoshop, Illustrator, QuarkXPress, Dreamweaver, GoLive, Flash, Final Cut Pro, and more. It's also packed with tips, tricks, and shortcuts for your favorite graphics applications.

http://www.macdesignonline.com

National Association of Photoshop Professionals (NAPP)
The industry trade association for Adobe® Photoshop® users and the world's leading resource for Photoshop training, education, and news.

http://www.photoshopuser.com

KW Computer Training Videos
Scott Kelby is featured in a series of more than 20 Photoshop training videos, each on a particular Photoshop topic, available from KW Computer Training. Visit the Web site or call 813-433-5000 for orders or more information.

http://www.photoshopvideos.com

Photoshop 7 Down & Dirty Tricks
Scott is also author of the best-selling book *Photoshop 7 Down & Dirty Tricks,* and the book's companion Web site has all the info on the book, which is available at bookstores around the country.

http://www.downanddirtytricks.com

Adobe Photoshop Seminar Tour
See Scott live at the Adobe Photoshop Seminar Tour, the nation's most popular Photoshop seminars. For upcoming tour dates and class schedules, visit the tour Web site.

http://www.photoshopseminars.com

PhotoshopWorld
The convention for Adobe Photoshop users has now become the largest Photoshop-only event in the world. Scott Kelby is technical chair and education director for the event, as well as one of the instructors.

http://www.photoshopworld.com

Photoshop Photo-Retouching Secrets
Scott is also the author of *Photoshop Photo-Retouching Secrets*. The book's companion Web site has all the info on the book and features downloadable source files for many of the projects. The book is available at bookstores around the country.

http://www.photoretouchingsecrets.com

Photoshop Hall of Fame
Created to honor and recognize those individuals whose contributions to the art and business of Adobe Photoshop have had a major impact on the application or the Photoshop community itself.

http://www.photoshophalloffame.com

VIEW CART 🛒   [   ] search ⊙

▸ Registration already a member? Log in. ▸ Book Registration

Publishing the Voices that Matter

OUR AUTHORS

PRESS ROOM

| web development | design | photoshop | new media | 3-D | server technologies |

EDUCATORS

ABOUT US

CONTACT US

You already know that New Riders brings you the **Voices That Matter**.

But what does that mean? It means that New Riders brings you the

Voices that challenge your assumptions, take your talents to the next

level, or simply help you better understand the complex technical world

we're all navigating.

Visit **www.newriders.com** to find:

- ▶ **10% discount** and **free shipping** on all book purchases
- ▶ Never before published chapters
- ▶ Sample chapters and excerpts
- ▶ Author bios and interviews
- ▶ Contests and enter-to-wins
- ▶ Up-to-date industry event information
- ▶ Book reviews
- ▶ Special offers from our friends and partners
- ▶ Info on how to join our User Group program
- ▶ Ways to have your Voice heard

New Riders

WWW.NEWRIDERS.COM

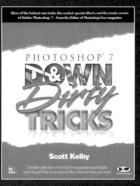